SURVIVAL IN THE SEA OF ECONOMIC CHAOS

SURVIVAL IN THE SEA OF ECONOMIC CHAOS

Perspectives on Leadership Actions for Businesses in Crisis

Carol L. Fatuzzo and **Ennio Fatuzzo**

PREFACE

E conomy in turmoil! Businesses in crisis! Is it over yet? Maybe, maybe not, or maybe the roller coaster of economic upturns and downturns is here to stay, becoming part of a new way of life. In any case, a recession or its aftermath is just one of many causes of economic problems for businesses. In our dynamic world, other giant waves of change are likely to sweep suddenly across the business landscape, altering everything in their paths.

Think about the other possibilities: earthquakes and tsunamis, political uprisings and revolutions, volatile oil prices, bankrupt nations, and more. Any one of these external forces can start the tremor that produces giant waves of economic chaos and business destruction. Such global disruptions are becoming the new norm. Thus surviving the resulting *"economic tsunamis"* and their destructive aftermath will be an ongoing challenge for business leaders in the 21ˢᵗ century.

We can say it another way. In today's world, whether or not there is an official recession, economic chaos remains. This "new reality", created by increasingly interconnected global economies, is unlikely to change, although the causes of the chaos may. What are the consequences? Businesses will continue to experience financial crises, frequently unanticipated and often created by events outside of their control.

How businesses can survive these crises and achieve stability in our turbulent world is the focus of our book "SURVIVAL IN THE SEA OF ECONOMIC CHAOS." And, as you will see in the coming pages, the key to business survival is effective leadership.

But not just any kind of leadership will do. In our fast–paced world, successfully combating business crises created by economic tsunamis requires a special kind of leadership—the kind that is decisive and adaptable to rapidly changing conditions. We call this *"Dynamic Business Leadership"* and devote the last part of our book to this subject.

The stage now is set: Businesses are adrift in the treacherous sea of economic chaos where survival depends on the leaders and their swift actions. What should these actions be, and what leadership qualities are needed? To find out, grab your life raft and sail along with us through the stormy business seas.

CONTENTS

PART TWO

PART THREE

CHAPTER 6

SURVIVAL IN THE SEA OF ECONOMIC CHAOS

*Perspectives on Leadership Actions
for Businesses in Crisis*

Introduction

Survival in the Sea of Economic Chaos

Economy in turmoil! Businesses in crisis!
The new normal for the 21ˢᵗ century.

O UR SUBJECT? Perspectives on different possible actions that the leaders of businesses struggling in the midst of economy–induced chaos could take. The causes of the chaos can range from recession to political revolution to tsunami to some other major disruptive event. But that doesn't matter. These are broad external forces beyond the control of any single business. What is important is that these forces can (and often do) have widespread economic impact. that cause crises for businesses. And these crises are likely to end in disaster without leadership intervention. So the focus of our book is business survival in difficult economic times, and we explore various leadership actions for achieving that goal.

OUR APPROACH? We start by describing results– oriented actions for quickly shoring up and stabilizing struggling businesses to help them "stay afloat" and cope with the financial crises created by external forces (i.e., recession, depression, or some other significant economic disruption). Then, as the turbulence eases and the economic environment improves, tactics and strategies for longer–term business survival and turnaround in performance are explored.

OUR "RECIPE" FOR SURVIVAL? There isn't any one "best" way of coping with the types of business crises caused by economic chaos. Therefore we: 1) suggest different types of leadership actions for different timeframes, 2) provide examples and easily accessible references that illustrate each type of action, and 3) describe different leadership, methodologies, and tools for optimizing decision–making, strategic and business planning, and implementation of chosen actions. In other words, we suggest approaches and alternatives.

However since there isn't just one right set of leadership actions or one best leadership approach, our book includes extensive references that provide more detailed information and offer differing perspectives on the actions we explore. Then, all things considered, we leave it up to you, the business leader, to choose the path that is most appropriate for your specific situation.

Now to create the proper mindset, we begin by describing what we mean by a *"business in crisis."*

A BUSINESS IN CRISIS

What is typical of businesses struggling in difficult economic times? Think of an economic downturn or a recession as a major "tsunami–like" disruption that sweeps across most businesses. Once a business is in the trough of its giant waves, everything seems to be falling apart. The business is "drowning" (failing).

Usually, under these circumstances, the current business plan isn't working and previously successful strategies are ineffective or obsolete. Programs aren't producing expected results. Product sales are low. Manufacturing costs are increasing not decreasing. Marketing and sales initiatives are ineffective. In conjunction with (or causing) these problems, there are multiple critical issues such as:

- Programs are behind schedule
- There is a shortage of cash for programs, including new product commercialization
- Manufacturing equipment is under–utilized
- Inventory is increasing
- Product and/or service pricing is no longer competitive

The end result? Business results are poor and goals are further away than before the "tsunami" and may be unattainable. Even business survival is in jeopardy. In other words, the business is in serious financial difficulty. Sales and profits are plummeting, and cash flow is decreasing or even negative.

The dynamics of how such a financial crisis usually develops are shown in *Figure I-1* on the next page. This simple plot shows dollars for both sales and profits over a period of time, starting just before the economic disruption and continuing after its onset (the vertical dashed line).

Specifically, as the economic "tsunami" approaches (left side of the plot), sales that had previously been growing begin to stall. And, slightly later, profits do the same. Then as the economy worsens, both sales and profits plummet (right side of the plot). This is a basic picture of a business in crisis, but is adequate for our purposes.

Declining Sales and Profits

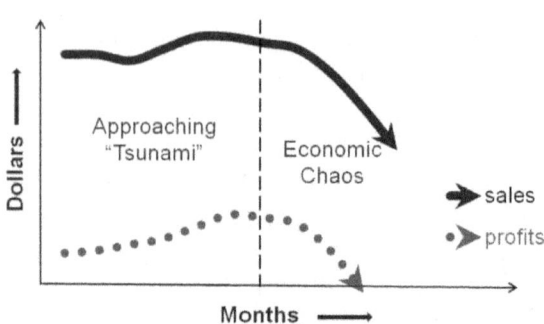

FIGURE I-1: THE FINANCIAL CRISIS

For an understanding of crises in more complex business situations, there are several books offering a more in–depth look at economic downturns and their impact on business (1).

Now, returning to the stage we have set. If a business leader recognizes in time an approaching financial catastrophe for his/her business, that leader has a number of options for making proactive changes to mitigate the situation. And, if the business has adequate cash reserves, there are additional possibilities.

However, it is often the case that sales and profits plummet in spite of initial leadership actions and that cash reserves are low. Then, the business is in a crisis situation. It is in the midst of an economic storm, and what we call *"Dynamic Business Leadership"* is a key requirement for survival.

DYNAMIC BUSINESS LEADERSHIP

What is *"Dynamic Business Leadership?"* To understand what we mean by this term, think about a business leader as the captain of a ship. When navigating in calm seas, the captain can reach the desired destination by relying on experience and direction from the stars. That approach is sufficient, even if the ship is old and fragile.

However, just to stay afloat in stormy and foggy weather, the ship has to be seaworthy; and the captain must be able to rapidly make and implement critical, life–saving decisions. The captain also needs to use modern navigation tools for frequent course corrections in order to have a reasonable chance of guiding his/her ship through the treacherous and unfamiliar waters and reaching shore intact.

In today's (and also most likely tomorrow's) disruptive economic environment, leading a business in trouble to "safe shores" is much the same. In crisis situations, a business leader must be decisive, adaptable, and able to make change happen rapidly. In addition, he/she must make use of the best information and management tools available in order for those actions to be effective. These characteristics are the key elements of what we call *"Dynamic Business Leadership."*

THE BOOK

As mentioned earlier, in our book we take a look at both the characteristics of dynamic business leadership and different possible leadership actions for combating crises. We investigate leadership actions in two timeframes:

1. *Immediate to short–term.* This timeframe encompasses those first actions focused on "keeping the business ship afloat" temporarily. The emphasis is on actions that can be implemented rapidly to make a positive financial difference and to provide some measure of financial stability.

2. *Intermediate to longer–term.* In this timeframe, a leader's actions must make sure that the business is "headed in the right direction" for survival, turnaround, and ultimately for growth. In other words, leaders must take action to guide their businesses toward safe shores.

In addition to the numerous references that are provided in both timeframes to explain the different actions that we introduce, we use several simplified examples of actual companies (not specifically identified) to illustrate the effect such actions can have in the real business world.

But to be effective in times of crisis, leadership actions must be the right ones and they must be timely. What is required is rapid, strategic decision–making and effective implementation of those decisions. How rapidly the changes must occur and how drastic the actions need to be depends on the magnitude of the crisis (or impending crisis).

So, how does a leader determine how quickly he/she needs to take action and how does he/she make the best decisions? To help leaders find answers to these challenging questions, we introduce and champion science–based methodologies and tools for business assessment and monitoring and for rapid strategic decision–making. We believe these types of tools are necessary foundations for business leadership in times of crisis.

In order to provide clear perspectives on leadership actions in different timeframes as well as leadership effectiveness, the book is divided into three parts.

Part One (*"Staying Afloat"*) focuses on short–term crisis abatement. It consists of two chapters:

CHAPTER 1 addresses *INTERNALLY–ORIENTED* actions related to core business activities. The goal is immediate cost/spending containment. These actions are temporary in nature, designed to reduce the company's burn rate and preserve working capital, and usually are easily reversible. Areas explored include discretionary spending, capital investments, and salaries.

CHAPTER 2 addresses Sales and Marketing related actions for improving the business financial situation, with a focus on existing products and customers. Actions discussed include pricing changes and promotions. These *EXTERNALLY–ORIENTED* actions generally can be implemented almost as rapidly as the actions discussed in

Chapter 1, but they may have longer–term implications.

Part Two (*"Heading in the Right Direction"*), addresses both internally–oriented and externally–oriented actions for the intermediate to longer–term horizon. Its two chapters explore tactics and strategies for continuing business survival and financial improvement. Specifically:

CHAPTER 3 considers intermediate–term actions, primarily with an *INTERNAL* focus, such as increasing organizational productivity, business rationalization, and business model revision. Since these are actions that may change the basic business structure or business itself, they need to be considered carefully before they are implemented.

CHAPTER 4 explores strategic choices both for turnaround and growth through business redirection. Actions considered include developing or acquiring new markets, products, or businesses. These types of actions (primarily having an *EXTERNAL* focus) usually require either cash or some sort of "partnering" but can be a key to business sustainability in the longer term—a time when the business landscape is likely to be considerably different than before the crisis occurred.

Part Three (*"Riding the Waves"*) is all about Dynamic Business Leadership:

CHAPTER 5 addresses putting together the actions from Chapters 3 and 4 in a coordinated thrust for business survival. To do this it first introduces various methodologies for decision–making and planning. It then illustrates how to use these "tools" to choose, plan, and implement specific actions for business survival. Additionally, it makes recommendations to business leaders for organizing, communicating, and effectively executing their chosen actions.

CHAPTER 6 provides a more in–depth look at the kind of leadership required in chaotic times. It focuses specifically on what we call dynamic business leadership. It describes the key elements of such leadership and champions the need for constant vigilance through the use of a "living" action plan.

To summarize, "SURVIVAL IN THE SEA OF ECONOMIC CHAOS" is all about timely and effective leadership actions for business stabilization and survival in a world that is continually changing due to disruptive external forces. But as you will discover, although we explore and propose a number of different types of actions for leaders to consider, we do *NOT* recommend any single direction to take. Why? Because every business is different, and every leader must make the best decisions possible given the specifics of his or her business crisis. We provide assistance in identifying alternative routes and understanding the terrain involved. Then it's up to the leader to use that information to guide the business to safe shores.

PART ONE

Staying Afloat

Crisis Abatement in the Short-Term

Chapter 1

Immediate Damage Control

The economy in turmoil! Your business in crisis! What should be done first? Chapter 1 focuses on triage for crisis abatement. The focus is *INTERNAL*. The actions laid out below are the first you should consider when your business is experiencing financial difficulty due to economic chaos. Which specific actions you should choose and how rapid and extreme those actions need to be depend on the severity of the crisis for your business; but it's a crisis so the quicker, the better.

Specifically, this chapter addresses actions to quickly reduce and control costs and spending. The goals are to minimize additional financial damage and, if you are lucky, to stabilize your financial situation. This chapter also takes a look at reducing cash expended through *MINIMIZING* (although not totally eliminating) Investments.

However, before taking any action, you need to have a clear understanding of the scope of the "damage." In other words it is important for leaders to quickly assess their business financial situation with some accuracy. A wrong assessment in such dynamic times can lead to actions that can be disastrous for the company. Therefore, this is where we begin.

ASSESSING THE BUSINESS FINANCIAL SITUATION

Damage Control first requires
quantifying the damage.

Rapidly making an accurate determination of your business financial situation is essential in times of economic chaos. In other words, it is critical to have a realistic understanding of the financial impact of the changing economy on your business. To develop a dynamic financial picture, we suggest focusing on simple metrics such as sales, profits, cash and cash flow. Then, for each of these financial measures, determine the present and the projected short–fall with respect to your current business plan.

To say it another way, first look at your business' past and current performance versus your forecast. Then, using this actual baseline, determine the expected short–fall in the next 6 to 12 months. You will need this information for the overall business, by segment, and by product in order to take appropriate corrective actions. If you would like additional information on business assessment, we recommend Chapter 2 in our book "DYNAMIC BUSINESS PLANNING BASICS" (2).

Once you have quantified the basic financial shortfall for your business, the next step is to focus on *INTERNAL* operations. A detailed analysis of costs/spending by category is needed to determine what area is having the largest *NEGATIVE* impact. This information provides the basis for your first actions. Later on, the focus will shift to understanding external contributors to your financial crisis such as the impact of the economic climate on your market, your competitors' actions, and changes in other external forces. This information will prepare you to take appropriate but somewhat longer–term actions. However first, as we have indicated, it's damage control by internal cost and spending containment and to do that, you need to quantify the "damage."

MEASURING PROGRESS

Increasing Cash Flow—the measure of success.

Once you have established your business financial baseline, including a detailed cost/spending analysis, you are almost ready to take action. However, it's important to be able to measure the impact of any actions taken on improving the business financial situation. Therefore, from this point on, we focus on *CASH FLOW* as a measure of business progress and/or success. In other words, we assume that the primary goal of any leadership actions in difficult economic times (particularly in the short term) is to increase the cash available to the company.

Why the focus on cash and cash flow? Simply, in difficult economic times, a company often fails because of a shortage of cash. In addition, those companies that have or can generate cash reserves are able to pursue business turnaround and *"game–changing"* actions even in the midst of economic downturns. These companies often emerge from the economic chaos as winners, not just survivors. Therefore, for businesses in the midst of economy–induced financial crises, increasing cash in the short–term is essential. (Note: increasing cash is important no matter what kind of disruptive event produces a financial business crisis.)

As we summarized in the introduction, we address two types of actions for increasing cash and achieving a positive operational cash flow—those having an *internal* orientation and those with an *external* orientation. And we consider different actions for different timeframes. However, whatever the timeframe and the type of actions chosen, one word of caution about measuring results (cash) is necessary. It is easy to fall into the trap of equating increasing sales to generating cash. Sometimes this is the case, but often it is not. So it is important to choose your metrics carefully. Note: Although financially–based actions (e.g., borrowing, refinancing, stock transactions) can affect cash and cash flow, this book does *NOT* address those. It focuses on actions that are based on operations and working capital.

If you would like to refresh your knowledge of cash flow, there are several internet references that provide good summary descriptions (3). And there are many books that provide a more in–depth look at cash flow and managing cash (4). In addition, we suggest the articles in Reference (5). These articles explain the importance of cash in difficult economic times and present summaries of various business strategies for combating economic downturns. In addition, they contain good examples of ways to both generate and preserve cash.

CONTAINING SPENDING/COSTS

*Cost–cutting doesn't have to be totally
disruptive to your business.*

Assuming that you now have detailed internal
cost/spending information, you are ready to take
appropriate immediate damage control actions. What
kinds of actions are best? Obviously it is those that will
have the biggest immediate positive financial impact
without seriously jeopardizing future business. But
there is a serious danger:

> *"Faced with mounting pressure to cut–costs,
> most companies continue to go about it the
> wrong way....They have defaulted to standard
> downturn defenses such as across–the–board
> cost–cutting and layoffs"* (6).

Why are general cost/spending containment
actions not the best ones? Basically, they can have
significant negative impacts on your customers and
your own organization; and they don't always produce
the magnitude of financial benefit anticipated.

But if across–the–board cuts, layoffs, and
general spending freezes are *NOT* the best actions,
what are the alternatives? We tackle the answer to this
question from two different perspectives. First we focus
on Organizational Spending. Then we consider
Operational Costs.

Organizational Spending

Some of the common categories to consider for
organizational spending containment actions include

discretionary spending, salaries, consultants, and education and training. These are areas where actions can be taken rapidly and will have an immediate effect on reducing spending and thus will improve cash flow. In addition, in most cases, these actions are quickly reversible when the financial situation rebounds, allowing you to return to more normal business operations. In other words, these cost–cutting actions are not totally disruptive to your business—if they are carried out in the right way.

First consider *discretionary spending*. This is a term that means different things to different people. For our purposes, we mean spending that is either non–essential or can be delayed or deferred without serious negative consequences. It includes areas such as travel, supplies, telephone expenses, dues and subscriptions, and awards. And you may have identified other important areas from your specific spending analysis.

Note: Although Research and Development (R&D) spending is sometimes considered discretionary, we recommend that you NOT consider it in this category. Our reasoning? We do not believe that R&D spending should be a candidate for immediate reduction because of the significant impacts such action can have on your business' eventual recovery. Instead, we consider R&D spending control as a survival tactic and address it as an intermediate–term action in Chapter 3.

But no matter what areas you consider discretionary, from your detailed business spending analysis you should have identified specific priority areas for focus—the ones that are the biggest cash drains. Appropriate and *SELECTIVE* cost containment actions should be fairly obvious, but a word of caution. Before taking action, remember to consider the potential impact of each action on your customers and on the productivity of your organization. Often spending cuts/freezes may be easy to dictate, but they can have serious negative consequences.

Next consider **salaries**. Immediate cost cutting related to salaries is not necessarily straightforward. First, we do *NOT* recommend considering the laying–off of permanent personnel in the immediate damage control phase. This is primarily because downsizing is not something that you can (or should) implement rapidly without detailed planning and analysis. In addition, downsizing has two major disadvantages:

1. The immediate financial impact is often less than anticipated because of factors such as severance packages.

2. It is difficult to hire high caliber, experienced personnel when business turns around since they are likely to have found other jobs.

However, there are business circumstances where downsizing is necessary. Therefore, we recommend that this type of action be considered as a survival tactic for the intermediate to longer–term and as such is addressed in Chapter 3.

What we do suggest considering first for immediate action related to salaries, is the reduction of temporary employees. However it is important to determine which specific temporary employees are non–essential and avoid taking sweeping actions such as termination of all temporary employees.

But, salary cuts and/or freezes relating to permanent employees do need to be considered. Again, across the board actions are *NOT* the best approach. But in this case, we do recognize that different legal and human resource considerations come into play. However, if possible, it is better to cut or freeze the overall salary budget but still keep rewarding excellence. In other words, be selective. Consider giving salary increases or one–time bonuses only to top rated employees. Although this approach may not provide the same magnitude of spending containment as across–the–board actions, this type of selectivity is much better for employee morale and productivity.

Now for the categories of **consultants** and **education and training**. For both of these areas, we suggest that you take a hard look at spending to determine what is nonessential and can be cut. In addition, there often are less expensive ways to accomplish the same goals that you should consider (e.g., distance learning, video conferencing, etc.). For both categories we again recommend selective cuts, not total elimination of spending.

Operational Costs

In this section we turn to cost containment actions relating to operations. Here we focus on actions not quite as easy or rapid to implement as those we have just discussed. Although there are others, the categories we focus on are Accounts Receivable, Inventory, and Lease or Rent expenses.

For **accounts receivable**, the actions are easy to list: monitor your accounts receivable, analyze your customers, and *stop supplying* *"unattractive"* *customers* (those that are slow paying and/or make only small purchases and/or yield unprofitable transactions for whatever reasons). It's easy to say, sometimes not as easy to do.

Next consider the area of **inventory**. Limiting inventory costs can have a big impact on cash flow. For example, special promotions/programs often can generate cash from slow moving or obsolete inventory. And decreasing the amount of inventory you keep on hand also offers benefits—if you can maintain an acceptable service level for your customers. Both of these types of actions usually can provide rapid results. Additionally, lowering material costs can have a positive impact on cash—whether through waste reduction or negotiating better prices from your suppliers. However these actions relating to material costs probably will take some time to implement. Additionally, you need to keep in mind that your suppliers also are likely to be experiencing financial pressures. Therefore you may wish to consider actions involving suppliers as short–term survival tactics.

Finally, we address **lease/rent expenses**. If applicable, try to reduce these kinds of expenses (e.g., buildings and/or equipment) by negotiating better rates, terminating leases, and/or outsourcing. Again, some of these actions will take time to implement and may involve unanticipated costs.

We end this section by repeating one more time: Whatever your business financial situation, if there is any way to avoid it, do *NOT* cut costs or spending across–the–board. And, whatever actions you are considering, be sure to realistically assess their actual

and specific impact on your organization, your
customers, and your business cash flow before
implementing them.

MINIMIZING INVESTMENTS

Sometimes some spending makes sense.

Minimizing investment spending in the short–term
could be considered as a part of cost/spending
containment; but this area, although it can provide
immediate and significant damage control, requires
different considerations due to the potential longer–
term impact of actions taken. Therefore, we treat
investments as a separate category. Further we have
divided investments into two kinds—Capital
Investments and "All Other" Investments.

Capital Investments

First, we address capital investments. For new capital
investments the general guideline is do *NOT* spend in
the short term. Often, significantly cutting (or
delaying) new capital spending is the single action that
can have the biggest rapid impact on cash flow. The
article *"Cutting Costs Without Drawing Blood"* (7)
provides a good perspective on this type of cost cutting.

But what about capital projects that already
are being implemented? Consider this situation: Your
Company is in the middle of a major capital project
when the economy changes, and now your business
financial results are plummeting. What should you do?
To address that question, we provide an example based

on a real company. Although recession is the cause of the business crisis in this example, the same questions and answers are applicable to businesses where financial crises are caused by the economic impact of other types of broad external forces.

THE RUBY CORPORATION: AN EXAMPLE

The Ruby Corporation owns/operates a national chain of upscale department stores. Before the 2008 recession business was growing rapidly, and the decision was made to open an additional store at a new location.

However, with the onset of the recession, the company's financial situation deteriorated (not unusual for recessionary times). Its revenues started decreasing while inventory increased resulting in decreased cash flow. Competitors began lowering prices and/or using aggressive promotions to gain business. In addition, Ruby's investment in a new store (expansion started before the recession) was not complete, although construction was in the final stages. In other words, some additional capital investment still was required to finish the structure. And, once the structure was completed, there would be additional costs associated with making the store operational.

So, the Ruby Corporation was faced with two important questions relating to capital:

1. Should they complete the new building—in spite of the additional investment needed?

2. If they completed the construction, should they open the new store for business—in spite of the recession and the company's weakening financial performance?

Consider first the construction. The depreciation for the capital investment already made would be charged to the business, whether or not the building was completed. Therefore there would be no significant financial benefit to the Ruby Corporation for stopping construction, and a completed building provides several options. However, in order to take this action, the needed cash must be available.

Now, what about the new store? Should Ruby go ahead and open it? The answer depends on factors such as the additional costs of operating the new store and the revenues it can generate *during the recession*. In addition, depending on its location, the new store may negatively impact one or more of Ruby's existing stores and/or may stimulate an aggressive competitive response. Both factors must be taken into account.

What actually happened? The building was completed, and the new store was opened. At the same time, Ruby closed several existing stores and reduced sales personnel at others. Overall, Ruby's financial position improved—probably due to a combination of actions, not just the new store.

The message from this example? Survival during an economic downturn is complicated and likely to require actions on several fronts. But even already initiated capital investments deserve careful scrutiny before spending decisions are made relating to them.

Non-Capital Investments

Now, what about non-capital investments? As far as these kinds of investments are concerned, whether the investment is in programs or people or something else, there is no blanket recommendation. The reasons for each investment need to be considered carefully before taking action. And it is important to keep in mind that if your business financial situation allows it (i.e., you have enough cash), continuing some level of investment in priority areas will increase your chances for longer term business sustainability.

General Conclusions

So, whether the investment is a capital one or some other kind, the situation is seldom black and white. However there are some general conclusions that can be made and that you should keep in mind when you are considering investing (or not investing) in difficult economic times. These are highlighted in *Figure 1–1*.

General Conclusions

New Capital Investments		
Are high risk in difficult economic times	Will have a significant, negative impact on cash flow	Should be avoided by businesses in financial difficulty

Other Selected Investments		
May be necessary to create a better future	Need to be carefully considered due to impact on cash flow	Should only be undertaken once the business is stabilized

FIGURE 1–1: INVESTING IN DIFFICULT ECONOMIC TIMES

For additional insight into ways to contain costs, including by minimizing investments, we suggest the articles and books in References (8) and (9).

Chapter 2

Rapid Defensive Moves

To protect and guide your business through a crisis, you need to complement your internal offensive actions with an aggressive, externally oriented defense—one that focuses on customers and competitors (i.e., marketing related actions). Why the focus on marketing? It's simple:

> *"There are only two things in a business that make money—innovation and marketing, everything else is cost." Peter Drucker (1954)*

The marketing related actions specifically addressed in this chapter are changes in pricing, sales promotions, and advertising spending. Generally, in times of economic downturns, these types of actions are reactions to the external forces that have produced negative changes in your business results. This makes them defensive in nature.

As was the case with the internally focused actions of Chapter 1, these types of defensive actions usually can be implemented quickly, and if done properly, can have a rapid and positive impact on cash flow. Conversely, the wrong moves can have a rapid negative impact, making your economy–induced business crisis worse or even fatal.

So what is right and what is wrong? That depends on your specific, current business situation (which was the first topic addressed in Chapter 1). But it also depends on the changes in your market induced by the economic chaos. We focus on both in this chapter as we explore possible "rapid defensive moves."

PRICING OPTIMIZATION

> *To decrease or not to decrease prices.*
> *That is the question.*

The first "rapid defensive move" we consider, and the one we explore in the most depth, is pricing optimization. In other words, what should you do with your prices in a depressed economy—decrease them, do nothing, or even increase them?

The general wisdom that you will find in the literature for difficult economic times is do *NOT* decrease prices (10). While this may be reasonable advice, it is not always the best course of action; and frequently it is not what your competitors are doing.

Depending on the uniqueness of your products and your competitors' actions, sometimes you should decrease prices and sometimes it actually is best to *INCREASE* prices. For example, consider the actions by Starbucks in the recessionary times of 2009 (11). In the fall of that year, the well–known coffee giant significantly increased prices on their specialty drinks while somewhat decreasing prices on their most popular beverages. With this combination of actions, Starbucks was striving to fend off lower priced competitors while improving overall business results.

As the article explains (11), increasing prices in the middle of a depressed economy isn't as crazy as it seems. It often can be an effective strategy for companies with premium products and high visibility.

However, what you should do depends on what you can or cannot afford to do based on the dynamics of your market, your cost structure, and what gives you an advantage *given the cost structure and actions of your competitors*. It also is important to keep in mind that, when your business is in a financial crisis, the short–term goal of pricing optimization is to *maximize positive cash flow*. And, as we explained in Chapter 1, this may not be the same as maximizing revenues.

Therefore the better question to ask is what, if any, pricing changes should you make? In other words, how can you optimize your pricing to increase the chances for business survival (i.e., maintain or increase market share and maximize positive cash flow)?

To answer this question you could seek guidance from the numerous marketing articles and books that cover in detail the subject of pricing. However these seldom address crisis situations where time is of the essence. Therefore we suggest using the practical, four step process summarized in *Figure 2–1* on the next page.

STEP 1 is all about Market Assessment. The objective is to determine how the dynamics of your market have changed (size, price sensitivity, demand for your specific types of goods and services, competitors) as a result of the economy. For example, in difficult economic times, markets typically shrink and/or become more price–sensitive and competitors become more aggressive. Also, the demand for luxury goods usually shows a larger downturn than the demand for more essential goods. In other words, as a starting point, you need to evaluate the impact of the economic climate, your competitors' resulting actions, and changes in other external forces on your Market.

Pricing Optimization Process

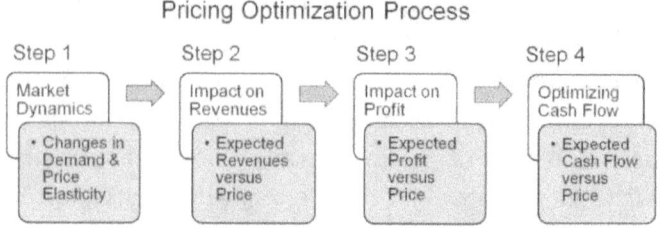

FIGURE 2–1: PRICING TO OPTIMIZE CASH FLOW

STEP 2 focuses on your Revenues (sales). First it is important to quantify the shortfalls for each different business segment and/or product. Assuming you have multiple businesses and/or products, you are likely to find that they are being affected differently by the depressed economy. Therefore the objective is to identify the segments/products that are the most and least impacted and attempt to determine the causes of the shortfalls (e.g., overall market changes, actions of certain types of customers, competitive actions, etc.). With this information you then can calculate your expected total revenues for specific products at various prices using the changed market dynamics. In other words, these expected revenues are based on your market assumptions relating to demand and price elasticity from Step 1.

STEP 3 deals with Profit. In this step you calculate expected profits for different possible prices.

However, before you can calculate profits, you need to understand your costs at various volumes, and these volumes depend not only on market dynamics but also on what your competitors are doing. Therefore it is important to consider the impact of competitive pricing/promotions on demand for your products. In other words, make sure that you understand in as much detail as possible what your competitors are doing or might do as a result of your actions and what impact that could have on your business. Once you have this information, you can calculate the effect of different prices on your expected profit.

In STEP 4, the conclusion of the pricing optimization process, the expected cash flow for different prices is calculated. With this information, the price which optimizes cash flow can be determined.

This 4–step process that we've described sounds simple, but how do you actually carry it out? To answer this question, we consider two cases: 1) where competition is not a significant factor and 2) where there is aggressive competition. In the first case we take the time to review fundamental supply and demand concepts because of their importance in dynamic economies. If you don't need this refresher, feel free to skip this section and move on to Case 2.

Case 1: "No" Competition

"No" competition assumes that the product is unique and/or protected by patents. Therefore, there will be no significant competitive response to pricing changes. This is the simplest case and provides a first step toward understanding the more complex situation when competitive actions must be considered. For this simple case, we assume that maximizing profit will also maximize positive cash flow (the short–term goal).

Of course at this point you could take the trial–and–error approach to optimizing pricing, but that takes time and is likely to make the situation worse. Therefore, the approach we suggest is quantitative and based on simple computer models to generate different data sets. Following are the details.

Step 1, as summarized above, is the market assessment. More specifically, for this "no competition" example, the focus is on the impact of the recession on market demand for the product. In order to determine this impact one must understand the economy–induced change in the demand versus price curve for the product (price elasticity of demand). This requires market research. Once you have this information, it is useful to plot it as shown below in *Figure 2–2*.

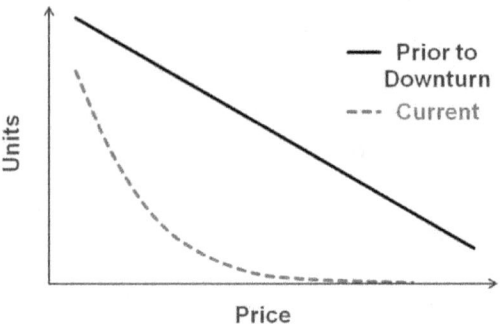

FIGURE 2–2: IMPACT OF ECONOMY ON PRICE ELASTICITY

In this figure Price is plotted on the x–axis with Demand (in units) on the y–axis for two timeframes— before the economic downturn and current. As you can see, this plot shows that the demand for the product changes significantly when the price is changed both before the recession and current. But it also shows that the shape and the displacement of the curves for the two timeframes are different. Why is that?

In generating the "current" curve, we have assumed that the overall demand for the product has significantly decreased as a result of the economic downturn (market size is smaller), and that it is more sensitive to price. This is often the case in depressed economic times, but you need to determine what your specific situation is.

Since you will have identified trends such as are shown in *Figure 2–2* but are unlikely to have exact data, it is useful to use a simple computer model to generate alternative demand curves based on your best estimates of the situation. This family of curves then can be used in Step 2 where you will determine your estimated total revenues for different price points.

For additional basic information on market dynamics, including price elasticity, see Reference (12). These are easily accessible internet articles. In addition there is a simple but clear explanation of price elasticity in Chapter 3 of "RECESSION STORMING" (13).

Now we turn to Step 2, still assuming "no" competition. In this step the impact of the changed market dynamics on revenues is quantified. More specifically, revenues for different possible prices are generated using the price versus demand curves from the Step 1. This can be done using the simple formula:

(Total Revenue at a specific price) = (specific price) X (the number of units you would sell at that price).

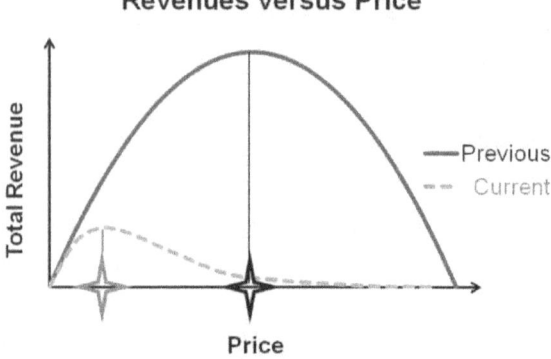

Revenues versus Price

FIGURE 2–3: IMPACT OF MARKET DYNAMICS ON REVENUES

Figure 2–3 (above) is an example of what the results might look like. Here we have plotted price versus revenue using the price elasticity curves shown in Step 1. The curves illustrate that overall current revenues have shrunk for all prices compared to the previous situation (prior to the economic downturn). In addition they show that the price that optimized your revenues before the downturn (black star) is not the same as the price that will optimize your revenues now (grey star). Obviously different market dynamics will produce different curves. Therefore again, for this step, using computer modeling to generate families of curves will allow you to rapidly assess the impact of different situations on your revenues.

If you stopped here, based on the situation illustrated in *Figure 2–3*, you probably would decrease your price. And ultimately that may be the correct move. However the goal is to optimize your *cash flow*, not revenues, so there is a need to move on to Step 3.

In Step 3, the information from Steps 1 and 2 is used, along with information on the product cost structure (manufacturing costs, sales costs, etc.), to create a picture of probable Net Profit at different price points. From this, a price point that optimizes Net Profit can be determined. *If nothing else has changed*, this price also optimizes positive cash flow.

More specifically, to determine the optimum price for maximizing net profit, you first need to quantify the fixed and variable costs for the specific product. Then, using this information, you can calculate "Total Costs" for different levels of demand (volumes). This is important since pricing changes will affect volumes and volumes usually affect cost. Specifically, the formula is: (Total Costs) = (Fixed Costs) + ([Units Sold] X [Variable Cost per Unit]).

Once you have determined the Total Costs for different volumes, you can calculate Net Profit for each price point using the Total Revenues from Step 2 and the formula: (Net Profit) = (Total Revenue) – (Total Costs). Again, plotting the results is helpful for decision–making, as we have done in *Figure 2–4* on the next page.

This figure illustrates what happens to profits as the selling price of products is varied in our hypothetical example. The detailed shapes and relative positions of your curves will be different depending on your specific business situation. However, assuming that the economic downturn has decreased the demand for your products and that demand for your products is sensitive to price, the curves shown in this figure, although somewhat extreme, do represent the general trends.

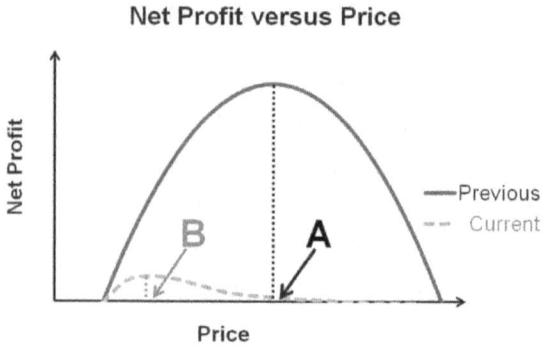

FIGURE 2–4: MAXIMIZING NET PROFIT

So what are these trends? First, look at the left side of the black curve in *Figure 2–4*. Here, the units sold increase as the price decreases, but the prices are so low that the revenues do not cover the costs. Therefore the profits decrease. Next, consider the right side of the curve. In this area, as the price increases, the units sold are decreasing. Again the revenues are too low to cover the costs, so profit decreases. The same is true for the left and right sides of the gray curve. Finally, compare the black (previous, before the downturn) and the dashed gray (current) curves. The contraction of the market has caused the gray curve to shift both down and left showing that you cannot sell as many units as you would have previously at any price point, and your fixed costs are more dominant.

The results? To maximize your profits, you need to *DECREASE* your price from the pre–downturn optimum (A) to the current situation optimum (B). This optimum price also will maximize your positive cash flow if price is the *ONLY* thing that has changed. However, if you have made additional changes (e.g., different payment terms or new capital investments) then maximizing profit may not be the same as maximizing cash flow. If this is the case, you need to take the additional step of calculating cash flow for each price point to determine your optimum price.

In addition, keep in mind that for this example we have focused only on quantitative factors such as cost and units sold for making pricing decisions. We have not considered other important factors like brand image and longer–term implications of price changes.

Case 2: Active Competitors

Next we consider the case with active competitors. The goal is the same: maximize positive cash flow through pricing optimization. But now this is a more difficult challenge. *Figure 2–5* summarizes some of the key additional factors that need to be considered.

FIGURE 2-5: COMPETITIVE FACTORS TO CONSIDER

However, in spite of these additional factors, the process to develop your pricing strategy is essentially the same. It builds on the same type of information that was collected for Case 1 (market dynamics and your revenues, costs and profits for different prices).

Consider first "*Demand Cross–Elasticity.*" This measures the effect on demand of goods from one supplier when another supplier changes its prices, assuming that the goods from one supplier can be substituted for those from the other. Commonly, when one company decreases the price, the demand for the substitute and now higher–priced competitive product decreases to some degree—to the benefit of the company that decreased prices. Therefore, when projecting your revenues at various price points, it is important to understand this aspect of your market dynamics. Using a computer to model the effects of different degrees of demand cross elasticity on demand, and thus revenues, is recommended. A key question to consider is: Is there enough demand cross–elasticity to enable you to gain market share from competitors with similar products by decreasing prices? For a review of basic information on demand cross–elasticity see Reference (14).

Next, it is important to consider "*Current Competitive Pricing/Promotions.*" In difficult economic times, companies often use aggressive pricing and promotions and unique approaches to customer service as survival tools. It is necessary to frequently monitor/verify what your competitors are doing in this respect in order to effectively combat those actions. Again, combined with the market dynamics information, simple computer models can help you explore the financial effect on your business of matching these actions or not.

Now, assess the probable impact of the economy on your *'Competitors' Sales and Profits"* (and their cash flow). Understanding the business financial situation of your key competitors often provides guidance as to the type and degree of actions that they may take of that you might want to consider. An extreme example would be a competitor that has reduced prices significantly but is about to declare bankruptcy. In this case, you probably would choose to wait before implementing price decreases.

That leave two additional key factors: *"Costs (fixed and variable)"* and *"Alternative Competitive Reactions."* Because understanding these areas can be more complex, we address them in more detail.

COSTS (FIXED AND VARIABLE)

In the final analysis, the financial advantage or disadvantage of price cutting depends on your total costs and those of your competitors. Therefore, *BEFORE* making any pricing changes, it is important to compare your fixed and variable costs at different levels of demand to those you assume for your competitors, based on competitive intelligence. This will allow you to understand volume/price constraints – yours and theirs.

Another way of saying this is that depending on the proportion of costs that are fixed versus variable, your total costs may change *in a different way* than those of your competitors as demand changes. Therefore, your pricing constraints and those of your competitors may not be the same. This needs to be factored into your pricing decisions. Since costs often are dominated by manufacturing costs, we focus on those to illustrate our point.

Below, in *Figure 2–6*, total manufacturing costs are plotted as a function of production volumes (units produced) for three possible production methods—fully automated (black dotted line), semi–automated (gray dashed line), and manual (black line).

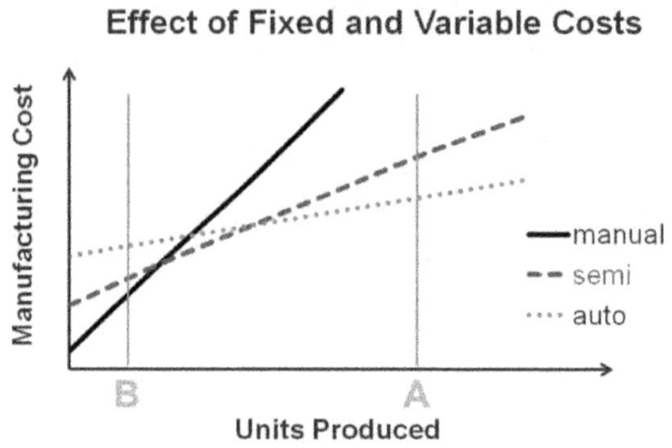

Effect of Fixed and Variable Costs

FIGURE 2–6: COSTS VERSUS UNITS PRODUCED

As the figure illustrates, in the case of a fully automated line, the fixed costs are high, but the variable costs are low, giving a manufacturing cost advantage at high volumes (A) and a disadvantage at low volumes (B). The situation is reversed for a manual operation (high variable costs and low fixed costs). It produces the lowest cost product at low volumes (B) but the highest cost product at high volumes (A). A semi–automated process lies somewhere in between.

What does this mean? In general, in good economic times when volumes are high, the company with the most automated process has the cost advantage. However, during a downturn, if volumes decrease enough because of lower overall demand, the cost advantage goes to the company with lower fixed costs (manual or semi–automated process).

How does this relate to pricing? If your manufacturing process is fully automated, you can gain market share profitably when demand is high (good economic times) by pricing your product lower than competition—just above your costs. Unless your competitors are equally automated, they will get into financial difficulty if they follow the same pricing strategy because their costs will be higher. During a downturn, assuming demand has decreased significantly, the situation is reversed. The same pricing strategy (price lower than competition and just above costs) now favors the least automated competitor.

What is your situation? It is not likely to be as black and white as our example, but these are factors that you need to consider before taking action.

ALTERNATIVE COMPETITIVE REACTIONS

It is just as important to consider *"alternative competitive reactions"* to your potential pricing changes. What is the best way to do this? *Figure 2–7* on the next page illustrates one way—the use of what we call *"qualitative"* Game Theory—to evaluate different scenarios.

This approach uses a simple matrix to provide a general picture of the possible alternatives. We call this *qualitative* because prices, sales, and profits are

NOT quantified. In other words, only general relationships are considered.

Your Price

	Lower	High
Competitor's Price — High	Competitor's Profit "LOWEST" / Your Profit "HIGHEST"	Competitor's Profit "Higher" / Your Profit "Higher"
Competitor's Price — Lower	Competitor's Profit "Medium" / Your Profit "Medium"	Competitor's Profit "HIGHEST" / Your Profit "LOWEST"

FIGURE 2–7: A "QUALITATIVE" GAME THEORY EXAMPLE

Specifically, *Figure 2–7* assumes that you and your competitor are selling a similar product manufactured on similar production equipment (i.e., price is the only differentiating feature) and that both of you have the possibility of charging a "high" or a "lower" price for your products *while maintaining profitability*. In other words, you and your competitor have similar cost structures. In this situation, your profits depend not only on your price but also on that of your competitor.

As *Figure 2-7* illustrates, you will have the "*highest*" net profits when you charge the lower price and your competitor charges the high price. This is because your market share (and thus units sold) increases significantly. And the reverse is true: "*lowest*" profit when you charge the high price and your competitor charges the lower one. And, you both will earn a "*higher*" profit when you both charge the high price and a "*medium* "profit when you both charge the lower price (no market share changes, so higher price means higher profit, lower price means lower profit).

So what price should you charge to maximize your profits (and your cash flow if nothing else has changed)? In difficult economic times, it is unlikely that both you and your competitor will choose to keep your prices high. Therefore, for this simple situation, your best decision is to charge the low price, which is also your competitor's best decision. And that competitor may have already taken action.

We have shown this example to emphasize how it can be useful to anticipate competitive reactions to your potential pricing changes before acting. In addition, it illustrates how qualitative Game Theory can be used as a simple way of gaining insight into alternative possibilities. But a word of caution is needed. Although it is easy to use, this approach can provide only general guidelines. It is inadequate for exploring complex competitive situations where many variables are important.

In real–life situations, actual numbers need to be used if you want to obtain more accurate predictions. For example, the conclusion drawn from our simple qualitative analysis is: "No matter what you competitor chooses for his/her prices, you are better off by charging low prices." However, if you use the same principles but more accurately model your real situation, you will find that the results depend on specific market dynamics and yours and your competitor's cost structures, as well as other factors (e.g. product differentiating features, value of customer service, etc.). Different numbers and different assumptions may favor quite different pricing strategies. This emphasizes the need to investigate several different price points as well as several different competitive scenarios.

In addition, in order to create a good strategy for pricing optimization (one that is realistic and accurate) in a complex real–world competitive environment, a more sophisticated computer modeling approach is recommended. For more information relating to Game Theory and other quantitative methodologies, including references, see Chapter 5.

General Pricing Guidelines

As you can see from the examples, pricing optimization is not simple in difficult economic times (or in any other time for that matter). However, as we stated earlier, much of the existing literature recommends *NOT* decreasing prices in depressed economies. But this "one size fits all" approach is too simplistic. Maintaining higher prices often is not realistic in the highly competitive environment of an economic downturn and does not always optimize cash flow.

To state this in another way, there are no black and white pricing rules for combating negative economic forces, but there are two critical goals: business survival and increasing positive cash flow. Based on these goals, for optimizing your pricing, we offer the general pricing guidelines highlighted in *Figure 2–8* on the next page. A few points related to these guidelines are worth emphasizing.

First, even if you have a unique or protected product, keep in mind the potential impact of price changes on "soft" factors like brand image and customer loyalty. Next, if you have competitors and they have already lowered their prices, don't automatically follow their pricing actions. As we state in the guidelines below (*Figure 2-8*), your business survival comes first. And finally, if prices have not yet changed, carefully consider possible actions by all involved before acting. Keep in mind that some of these actions may have nothing to do with pricing.

General Pricing Guidelines

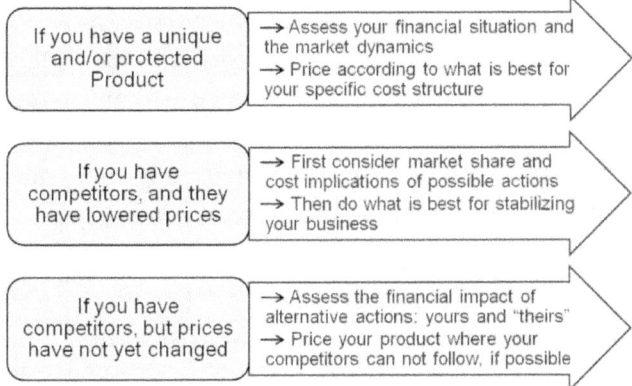

FIGURE 2–8: OPTIMIZING YOUR PRICING

To repeat, pricing optimization, particularly in difficult economic times, is a complex topic. One useful summary of key factors to consider can be found in the blog "*Pricing Strategies for the Downturn*" (15). In addition, you can find general information on pricing in internet articles such those in Reference (16). And, if you would like more in–depth information, we suggest the books in Reference (17).

SALES PROMOTIONS

There are alternatives to
"permanent" price decreases.

So far we have explored pricing changes (often decreases) as rapid, customer–focused actions for generating cash. However, whether intended or not, price decreases tend to be permanent. In other words, at the end of a downturn it is difficult to raise prices and still retain market share.

But there are alternatives to such "permanent" price decreases, and these alternatives are sales promotions. These types of marketing/sales programs can take many different forms, but all offer customers temporary incentives to entice them to purchase products and, if successful, can generate cash rapidly. But are such programs really a good idea?

To answer that question, think about the types of promotional incentives that can be offered. These include the obvious such as discounted prices (temporary price decreases). However there are many other possibilities such as free shipping, special/free gifts, buy–one–get–one–free, bundling, bonus points or coupons, and finance deals. And these are just a few of the different sales incentives that are becoming common. There are many clever variations on each of these to entice customers to purchase products.

But do these types of tactics truly increase cash flow in the short term? And what are the somewhat longer term financial and/or other implications for your business? In other words do they indeed generate additional cash over and above the "normal" cash being generated by the business?

To address these questions, we consider some of the potential advantages and/or disadvantages of using sales promotions.

Advantages:

- Time Value of Money. If cash is needed *NOW*, even at the expense of cash later, promotions may be an excellent strategy and provide real cash flow advantage.

- Temporary market share gain. Depending on competitive responses, a promotion may increase your sales at the expense of your competitors, thereby temporarily increasing your market share and cash flow.

- Net cost decrease. If your fixed costs are high, a promotion can increase your volumes thereby decreasing your overall costs per unit and increasing your cash flow.

Potential Disadvantages:

- Profit decrease. A sales increase at a lower price can result in a net profit decrease, and thereby provide less cash than would have been obtained without the promotion.

- Overall Sales reduction. The immediate increase in sales due to the promotion may be at the expense of sales (and cash) when the promotion ends (i.e., promotional sales are only those that would have occurred anyway but in a later timeframe).

- No additional sales. It is possible for there to be NO increase in sales. So, the same numbers of units are sold at a lower price producing lower profits and less cash.

- Competitive reaction. Assuming that you have competitors, they are likely to react aggressively to your promotions and everyone may loose from a cash flow standpoint.

So, should you consider a promotional strategy? The answer is "it depends." You need to accurately calculate the likely *NET* effect of the promotion on cash flow both during and after the promotion. To minimize risk and maximize benefit, other types of promotions (those not based purely on price) should be considered. These may provide different and more attractive cost/cash advantages than purely price–based promotions.

As an example, consider "free shipping." Free shipping was one of the major strategies to drive online retail sales during the 2010 holiday shopping season (November–December). And it seems to have worked. 2010 holiday web dollar sales were up by more than 15% percent compared to those of the 2009 season.

In contrast, 2010 in–store holiday sales showed only a modest increase of about 3 percent compared to the 2009 holiday season (18). So, free shipping may not have been the only factor, but it seems to have been at least a key influence in driving traffic.

What actually happened? International mega–retailer Wal–Mart took the lead in offering free shipping for online purchases (19), but they certainly weren't alone. Toys R Us, Williams–Sonoma, Target and J.C. Penney (just to mention a few) also offered this "no–charge" incentive. And of course, Amazon.com has been offering unlimited two–day free shipping for a modest annual fee for quite some time.

So the big question became: What's next? Will shoppers continue to expect incentives such as free shipping? Steve Nave, senior vice president and general manager of Walmart.com, told The New York Times that it's a trend that he predicts will turn into a standard. "I would expect to see us continue to have offerings similar to this in the future in some way, shape or form," he said (19). So, bottom line, free shipping for the holidays appears to have been a successful "temporary" price reduction tactic that wasn't really so temporary.

What about examples of other promotional strategies? The internet articles in Reference (20) describe a few different kinds of sales promotions and pricing strategies, both often mixed together. These include incentives such as discounts to new customers, bundling, coupons, "stripped down" products at "affordable" prices, and more.

ADVERTISING SPENDING

> "Some companies reduce MarCom spending significantly. (They go dim.) Others virtually pinch ... spending to a mere trickle. (They go dark.) But spending money in an economic downturn can...contribute to...profits" (21)

In this section we explore one additional customer and market focused area where appropriate actions can rapidly generate cash: changes in advertising (or marketing communications) spending. We have already discussed delaying Capital investments, so why not just cut/delay advertising spending as well to increase cash flow? There is mounting evidence that this is a dangerous move as the article quoted in the beginning of this section explains well.

In addition, there are several detailed articles providing quantitative marketing evidence that *INCREASING* advertising expenditures during economic downturns offers opportunities to increase market share as well as producing both short and long term financial benefits (22). You also may find the article "When the Going Gets Tough, the Tough Don't Skimp on Their Ad Budgets" (23) thought–provoking.

But your business is in crisis, and you are not convinced that marketing studies based on past recessions and downturns apply to your situation. So what should you do?

Before deciding to simply cut advertising spending as a part of your cost containment actions, it is important to keep in mind the business survival goal—increasing short–term cash flow. Assuming that your advertising dollars have been responsible for producing good results (increasing profits), cutting advertising spending may reduce profits more than it reduces costs, thereby decreasing cash flow. So what is best? There are three possibilities.

First, you could *INCREASE* overall advertising spending. If you have the cash and are reasonably sure that the increase in profits will be significantly larger than the increased spending, this can be a good strategy, even in difficult economic times. However, assuming that there are multiple products involved, it is usually the case that not all advertising spending is equally effective. Therefore selective increases will be a better choice than across–the–board actions.

Second, you could *MAINTAIN* your current advertising spending at its current level. But again, it is unlikely that all of your advertising spending is equally effective, so if you have the cash to keep spending at the same level, you should at least consider a different distribution of that spending.

Finally, you could *DECREASE* your overall spending. This may be your only choice, but you need to carefully consider the specifics of your current spending to decide where to cut and how much. Wrong actions can rapidly decrease cash flow, making your situation worse. As we emphasized in Chapter 1, it is seldom best to make across the board cuts.

So how should you proceed? As with most marketing focused cost containment actions, the right decision for your business depends on many factors such as your specific products, your customers, your competitive position, and changes in your market dynamics—all a part of the financial and market assessments we explored earlier. Therefore, assuming that your business involves multiple products, we recommend the following sequential steps:

1. Assess the effectiveness of your current advertising spending by product

2. Use that information along with other relevant data to prioritize your current advertising programs

3. Project the effects of increasing, redistributing, and/or reducing your advertising spending according to those priorities

4. Then take the appropriate action

A graphical approach to this prioritization and redistribution process is shown below in *Figure 2–9*.

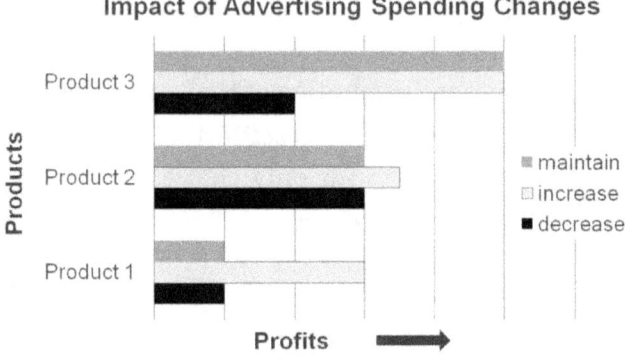

FIGURE 2-9: PRIORITIZING ADVERTISING EXPENDITURES

This chart compares the expected impact of different levels of advertising expenditures on the profits for different products. With this kind of *semi-quantitative* information, you can make some general observations such as:

- Product 3 is a candidate to leave alone. (Increased spending has no effect on profits, but decreased spending has a large negative effect.)

- Product 2 is a candidate for decreased spending. (Decreased spending has no effect on profits, increased spending has only a minor effect.)

- Product 1 is a candidate for increased spending. (Increased spending increases profits significantly.)

This approach provides some general guidance. However, it is important also to compare *quantitatively* the current level of advertising spending for your products and the profits it produces. In other words, what is your current return on advertising dollars for each product? Then you can answer for each product the specific questions: Is the amount of advertising spending worth it? How much additional spending would be required to significantly increase profits? How much could be saved by cutting spending?

And one final factor to consider as you prioritize your spending: How important is the product to your business? Then, it's up to you to use all of this information to make the best decisions for your business on how to redistribute and focus your advertising spending to maximize your cash flow.

You may find it helpful to take a look at what other companies did in the 2008 recession. The internet articles in Reference (24) provide examples and specific suggestions. And there is one final recommendation. Before taking action, it may be worthwhile to take a look at some of the detailed marketing information that we referred to earlier (22) because these data show that the effects of increased advertising spending in difficult economic times vary by industry and by type of business. In addition, for more general information on how to market in an economic downturn and some different perspectives, see the internet articles in Reference (25).

PART TWO

Heading in the Right Direction

*Survival Actions for the
Mid/Longer Term*

Chapter 3

Survival Tactics for the Mid-Term

In Chapter 3 we once again focus on the internal business organization, but now we address survival actions for a somewhat longer timeframe than the more immediate and rapid actions discussed in chapters 1 and 2. Like those in earlier chapters, the actions covered in this chapter may involve cost cutting. But unlike those previous actions, the survival tactics that we explore here usually have longer–term, strategic implications and often are irreversible.

Specifically covered in this chapter are actions focused on personnel and operations (increasing organizational productivity, including downsizing) and actions affecting the basic business framework (business rationalization and business model changes).

In addition, although R&D (Research and Development) spending optimization could have been addressed in Chapter 1 under immediate cost containment, it is included in this chapter. This is because of the significant impact this type of action can have on a business' eventual recovery and because R&D spending related actions may not involve cost cutting at all. Instead, the actions may focus on a redistribution of resources to maximize the near–term impact of selected programs.

When considering the types of survival actions dealt with in this chapter, it is important to address general questions such as:

- How big are your financial problems? Are layoffs or downsizing a good option? Should you make across–the–board cuts or should cost cutting be selective (the hatchet versus the scalpel approach)?

- Will your actions really affect your cash flow positively in the short–term?

- What will be the impact of your actions on your business' future?

- Are you using the best available information, methodologies and tools for your decision–making?

Exploring answers to these questions will be a common thread throughout this chapter.

ORGANIZATIONAL PRODUCTIVITY

> *Productivity! The challenge of*
> *doing more with less.*

Our first set of "tactics" for business survival is focused on increasing organizational productivity. If successful, these kinds of tactics address the seemingly contradictory challenge of *doing more with less*. There are three general productivity improvement areas that we investigate here: organizational restructuring, improving functional operations, and outsourcing.

Organizational Restructuring

Restructuring, with a focus on infrastructure changes, is the first kind of survival tactic that many business leaders consider when seeking to increase productivity and reduce costs. And to most, this term means downsizing.

Downsizing. Layoffs. Restructuring. Whatever you call it and however you do it, if the goal is major personnel reduction, then these actions are cost cutting with a long–term strategic impact. What are the pros and cons of such drastic survival tactics?

THE ADVANTAGES: Major reductions in spending are possible.

THE DISADVANTAGES: Cash flow benefits, particularly in the near–term, may not be as large as anticipated due to factors like separation packages and fixed costs. In addition, the expertise and experience lost may be difficult to replace when the economy improves, affecting the ability to achieve a "turnaround" in business performance.

THE REALITY: Significant downsizing may be your only path to survival. And this kind of "restructuring" is a common way companies cope with financial crises, whether or not they are economy–induced.

As an example, *Figure 3–1* on the next page graphically illustrates a small sampling of company layoffs resulting from the 2008 recession. If you search the Internet it is easy to quickly add more names of companies that aggressively have used layoffs as a "survival tactic" in difficult times—Dell, Macy's, Office Depot, Target, Wal–Mart, and the list goes on.

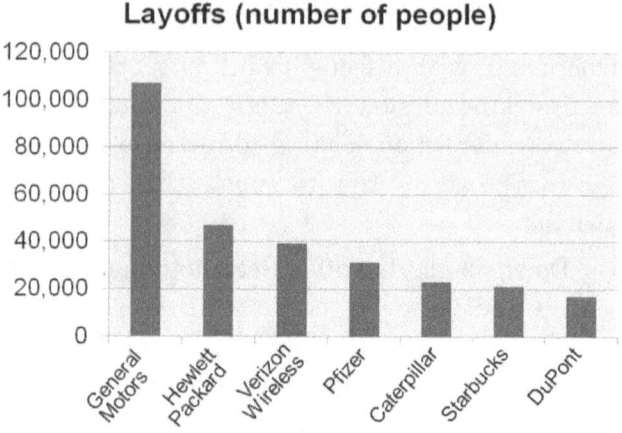

FIGURE 3–1: LAYOFFS – 2008/2009 (26)

The point is, in challenging economic times, businesses of all kinds and sizes judge it to be necessary to resort to downsizing to cut costs and increase organizational productivity and hence cash flow.

So, some form of downsizing may be your only or your best option for survival and business stabilization. But how do you decide? No book can tell you how to proceed or list rules to follow. Anything more than general guidance depends on the specific business financial and strategic situation. However the internet articles in Reference (27) do provide different and thought–provoking perspectives on downsizing that you might want to consider. In addition, the book "RESPONSIBLE RESTRUCTURING: CREATIVE AND PROFITABLE ALTERNATIVES TO LAYOFFS" (28) also provides some useful insights. Our advice? If you decide downsizing is necessary, consult expert resources and plan carefully *BEFORE* acting so the cash flow benefits you obtain are what you expected.

But downsizing is not the only kind of organizational restructuring that can increase productivity and cash flow. There are other kinds of actions that can have significant impacts. We highlight three examples: re–organization, business process streamlining, and information technology.

RE–ORGANIZATION

First consider *re–organization*. Costs may be cut by actions such as combining divisions or departments, reassigning responsibilities, and/or selectively eliminating a few personnel (e.g., middle management). Or, if some parts of the organization are significantly over– or under–resourced (staffing and/or dollars), making appropriate adjustments can lead to positive results.

These are just a few examples of change through re–organization. If these types of changes are made correctly, they can lead to improved communication and clearer accountability for results. The end results of all of this: Increased efficiency, effectiveness, and cash flow.

BUSINESS PROCESS STREAMLINING

Next, think about *business process streamlining*. A business process can be defined as a series of tasks to be completed, by people, to achieve a specified purpose. It also includes the systems that support the tasks.

Business process streamlining is all about finding ways of completing these tasks in a better and faster way. For example, what is your approval process? Is it a roadblock to completing a task? Can it be simplified and happen faster? And what about your projects? Are cost savings programs producing the needed results in a timely fashion? Are products being commercialized rapidly enough and producing needed revenues? If not, perhaps changes to the processes used for managing and tracking projects are in order.

These are just a few examples of business process streamlining that can lead to improved financials—assuming that the things that end up being done faster and better are the right things to be doing.

INFORMATION TECHNOLOGY (IT)

And finally, think about *information technology* (computers, software, etc.). There are the obvious productivity advantages to using Information technology (IT) such as the ability to quickly obtain competitive and market information from internet searches and individual productivity increases through the use of tools such as email, video conferencing, and word–processing.

In addition, new technology and innovative use of computer–based capabilities can produce significant changes in workflow and production processes. In other words, the automation of various business tasks and processes can contribute significantly to business process streamlining.

Bottom line, organizational restructuring through the expanded use of IT often can provide significant productivity and financial benefits.

Improving Functional Operations

In this section we consider the business Functions (Research and Development, Manufacturing, Marketing, Sales, etc.). Increasing the efficiency and productivity of each individual Function is the first step towards operational improvement. There are many ways to approach this goal depending on your specific business situation. However one key issue that often needs attention is human resources. Having the right skills, expertise, and experience in the organization and the right people in the right jobs can have a major positive impact. Since this is an area most business management is familiar with we won't dwell on it here. Our advice: *TAKE ACTION.* Make the changes that you know are necessary.

Now for a different perspective on Functional operations. Although productivity improvements are important for improving the operations of each Function individually, just as important is what we call "*Functional alignment.*" What is Functional alignment? It consists of several pieces.

First, the plans and projects of each Function must support the overall business plan and priorities. In other words, each activity of each Function must be aligned with the goals and strategies of the business.

But Functional alignment is more complex than having common goals and strategies. Although each Function separately is a critical element of the business, no Function operates in isolation. Therefore, for optimum operational and business performance (efficiency and effectiveness) it is essential that each Function's plans be integrated with the plans of the other Functions. In addition, each Function's actions must take into account the other Functions' actions and constraints (skills, equipment, cash, etc.). Continuing communication and feedback among the Functions are required for achieving this level of alignment.

This multi–faceted integration of plans and actions is what we call Functional alignment. When accomplished, it ultimately leads to high–performance, coordinated business teams and can produce large benefits in organizational productivity and ultimately cash flow.

Outsourcing

The last area we focus on for increasing organizational productivity is outsourcing. Very simply, outsourcing can be defined as the contracting out to external providers of services and/or processes currently performed in–house. If these external providers are in another country, this is commonly referred to as "offshoring".

In our definition, we also include the temporary action of "subcontracting" a specific task as a part of outsourcing. This type of outsourcing includes contracting out segments of activities such as the manufacturing of components of products or the development of a specific technology or the completion of a specific project or the selling of products to a particular market segment. But it also might involve contracting out entire functions. Outsourcing of manufacturing gets most of the attention in this latter category, but outsourcing services like finance, legal, sales, or even research can provide significant benefits.

Why consider outsourcing? There are many reasons beyond the obvious one of labor savings:

"True, the labor savings from global sourcing can still be substantial. But it's peanuts compared to the enormous gains in efficiency, productivity, quality, and revenues that can be achieved..." (29)

So yes, outsourcing is a way to cut costs through labor savings. But it isn't only about layoffs and cutting costs. Outsourcing, done properly, also provides companies with many other benefits such as:

- Increased focus on Core Business (more resources available)
- Cost restructuring (i.e., changing a fixed cost to a variable cost, and making variable costs more predictable).
- Access to operational expertise (i.e., provides access to operational best practices that would be too difficult or time consuming to develop in-house such as specialized IT services)
- Access to a larger talent pool and a sustainable source of specialized skills
- Improved capacity management, including shifting the risks of dealing with increases or decreases in production to the supplier.
- Reduced time to market (e.g., acceleration of the development/manufacture of a product through additional capability from the supplier)
- Cost–effective access to services which usually are available only to large corporations
- Avoidance of capital investments

In other words, outsourcing can provide not only financial benefits for business survival in the near–term, but also competitive advantage for business turnaround in the longer–term.

Increasing organizational productivity through restructuring, improving functional operations, and outsourcing. That's what this section has been all about. The message? The right kinds of organizational changes in areas such as those we have described can provide cash flow increases through what end up being essentially cost reductions. Generally, if these changes do not involve significant downsizing or outsourcing, they are not too disruptive to your business and allow you to preserve the ability to rebound when the economic situation improves.

Therefore, unless your business is facing imminent "death", we encourage you first to look carefully at your organizational structure, operations, and business practices. Often simple changes in these areas can have a large positive impact. For additional perspectives and detailed analyses of ways to increase organizational productivity, see Reference (30).

BUSINESS RATIONALIZATION

Leave those dead weights behind!

The next survival tactic we address is Business Rationalization. If, after a detailed analysis of your business' financial performance, you find products and/or markets and/or businesses that are producing poor financial results, *leave those dead weights behind*! In other words, you should consider actions such as:

- Discontinuing the selling of the low–performing products (unless they have a strategic reason to exist or unless customers are prepared to keep buying at an increased price or unless the cost of exit is so high that it would have a negative cash impact that you can't afford)

- Exiting unattractive Market and/or Business Segments (unless they have a strategic reason to exist or unless exiting will seriously handicap your chances for business turnaround)

- Discontinuing projects or selling off products and/or businesses outside of your core competency areas (unless you have the means to build/gain those core competencies)

But as is sometimes the case with actions for productivity improvement, actions oriented towards significant business rationalization often must be accompanied by downsizing in order to achieve the cash benefits. Only a detailed financial analysis can help you make the right decision.

However it is important to keep in mind the strategic impact of any business rationalization actions and their effect on the potential for your business recovery and growth as the economy improves. To emphasize this point, we use an example—The Amber Corporation.

SURVIVAL CHOICES: THE AMBER CORPORATION

The Amber Corporation is an established company that has been in business for a number of years. The company develops, manufactures and sells a broad range of household furniture products, from standard low–priced items (high volume products) to high–priced specialty products (low volume products).

Until the economic downturn both profits and growth were good. But then the situation changed. Basically, the overall demand for household furniture products decreased due to the economy, and price sensitivity increased. As a result, the sales of all of Amber's products fell and inventory started increasing. However there was a larger negative effect on Amber's previously highly profitable specialty products. Cash flow started decreasing.

To make matters worse, a new competitor appeared that was selling products similar to Amber's standard products but at a lower price. This caused Amber to start losing market share. Unfortunately, due to Amber's cost structure, any decrease in the prices of its standard products would further decrease cash flow.

What did Amber do? Amber's Chairman decided to retreat from its high–volume standard furniture business (i.e., to exit the larger but less profitable segment) and to retrench to the niche business of higher–priced and more profitable custom products. This significant business rationalization involved closing Amber's largest manufacturing plant and laying off a significant number of employees, making it almost impossible for Amber to re–enter the standard product business segment at a future time. But *what was left* of Amber's business survived.

Was this choice of limited survival today at the expense of future business the right one? It's hard to answer that question without additional information, but Amber could have made other tactical survival choices.

For example, instead of exiting the entire segment, Amber could have discontinued only the poorest performing standard products (e.g., high cost, low profit, low volume). Or, to lower product costs, the company could have outsourced the manufacturing of standard products (or all products). However this alternative would have required finding and contracting with an organization having the appropriate capability and cost structure. Amber also could have formed an alliance with a low–cost furniture manufacturer and sold that manufacturer's standard products at competitive prices. Again this option depends on finding a suitable partner.

And there are still other survival alternatives that Amber could have considered such as:

- Changing the distribution/sales approach (using a contract sales force, selling direct instead of through distribution, etc.)
- Selling selected standard products to related markets to keep volumes high and costs low (Offices, hospitals, restaurants, etc.)
- Forming a "partnership" with a company already offering other products to Amber's customer base and selling both set of products
- Using their excess manufacturing capacity to manufacture products for others (assumes that Amber's capabilities were in demand and that they had the right cost structure)

Did Amber consider any of these? We don't know. Would any of these have been better? That's a question that is impossible to answer without further details on the cost structure of the business and other relevant constraints. Perhaps a combination of business rationalization and some of the alternatives that we have listed would have allowed Amber to generate needed cash without significant layoffs or business downsizing. But there is no certainty. As we said in the beginning, for a business in crisis there is no one path to survival—just alternatives to carefully consider.

What is the point of this example? Business rationalization to some degree can be an important survival tactic, but taken to an extreme it usually limits future business possibilities. Therefore, before heading down that path, it is important to consider alternative tactics or combinations of tactics that offer the potential for near–term financial benefit while preserving the possibility of business turnaround in the longer–term. However many of the tactics that can accomplish this (such as those we listed in the Amber example) involve making fundamental changes to the way you do business. In other word, business model revision is required—our next topic.

BUSINESS MODEL REVISION

How should you "do" business to survive?

Why is business model revision an important action for you to consider? Your business model provides the framework for the way you currently do business, but it also defines your business constraints. Therefore revising or changing this framework can sometimes be a key to business survival and eventual turnaround. In other words, by being creative in the way you "play" the business game and/or add value for your customers, you often can gain competitive advantage and improve your business situation. The first step toward this goal is clearly defining your current business model. Then you can consider revising it.

Business Model – A Definition

What is a business model? Simply, a business model describes how you bring products (including services) to life, how you deliver value to customers and entice them to pay for that value, and ultimately how you profit from these products. This description of the way you do business is your baseline. More specifically, by answering two basic types of questions you can clearly define your business model. These questions relate to your business operations and your value proposition.

The first type of questions deals with how you currently do Business:

Sourcing: How do you "obtain" the products you sell? Do you outsource R&D and/or manufacturing, do you sell products obtained from someone else, or do you do everything yourself?

Distribution: How do you reach your customers? Do you have your own sales force, sell through distribution, do business over the Internet, or do you use some combination of approaches?

Partnerships, Customer Relationships: Do you rely on any special alliances or relationships with customers, "middlemen" or decision makers?

Revenue flows: How do you generate profits (make money)? What are the revenue streams and what is your cost structure?

The second type of questions defines your framework for creating value. Here the key question is: *What benefits do you offer your customers?* Typically the answers include things such as product performance and price, response time, customer service, and social value (e.g., green).

For more detailed descriptions of business models as well as examples, see Reference (31). In addition, the article *"Why Business Models Matter"* by J. Magretta (32) provides an in–depth look at business models and their importance.

Now, once you have clearly defined your business model (i.e., have answers to the basic business model questions) you can address revising part of this framework to improve your finances and/or change your competitive situation.

Revising Your Business Model

How should you approach revising your business model? Think about how you might do business differently. Consider questions such as: How else could you "obtain" the products you sell? In what other ways could you reach your customers? Are there any special alliances or other relationships that could make a difference? Is there a way to change your revenue streams and/or your cost structure for growth and financial benefit? What else could you change in your business framework to make a difference?

Or, you could consider offering new services and/or ways to benefit from others' products and services. This might include things such as:

- Providing new services related to your existing products
- Obtaining new products and/or services to offer for sale through acquisition, partnership, or some other sort of business arrangement
- Selling products for others using your distribution network
- Making products for others using your manufacturing capability

As you probably recall, these are the kinds of alternatives that we briefly described in the Amber example. And, just like business rationalization, they are likely to change your business irreversibly.

Therefore, before making these kinds of business model changes, it is important to take into account your current business situation and thoroughly evaluate the financial impact of doing business differently. This includes assessing competitive reactions, identifying any gaps in your core competencies, and making plans to close those gaps. Considering factors such as these is particularly important when possible actions involve providing new services or acquiring new products or businesses.

So, should you revise your business model? Obviously that decision is up to you, the leader.

However many companies have taken this kind of action and benefited from it. For current examples (Dell, Amazon, and Apple), see Reference (33). In addition, the articles and books in References (34) and (35) provide a variety of examples and different perspectives on the importance of business models, new types of business models to consider, and the benefits that can be gained from changing your business model in chaotic economic times.

R&D SPENDING OPTIMIZATION

Minimize near–term cash investment without killing the possibility of future growth.

Now we take a look at R&D programs and the associated resources. We focus on those programs where new products and technologies are being developed, but the general principles and actions that we describe can be applied to any kind of program.

The survival tactics we explore are ways to cut and/or redistribute R&D spending. The goal is to focus resources in a way that has the most impact on minimizing near–term cash investment *WITHOUT* killing the possibility of future business prosperity.

The first and most important step toward achieving this goal is prioritizing R&D programs. This provides the framework for making intelligent choices with respect to where to make cuts and how to redistribute resources. Therefore, we address program priorities first, and then consider spending changes.

R&D Program Prioritization

There are various ways to prioritize R&D programs, but they all start with program evaluation. One accepted approach to this is described in the article *"Is It Real? Can We Win? Is It Worth Doing?"* by G. Day (36). Although this article was written during "calm" economic times, the methodology is just as relevant for program evaluation in times of economic chaos. Then, the book "PORTFOLIO MANAGEMENT FOR NEW PRODUCTS" by R. Cooper, S. Edgett, and E. Kleinschmidt (37) addresses moving from program evaluation to program prioritization.

Both of the above references describe a number of specific prioritization criteria. However, in difficult economic times, three of these have increased importance. As *Figure 3–2* below illustrates, these are cash needs, timing, and risk.

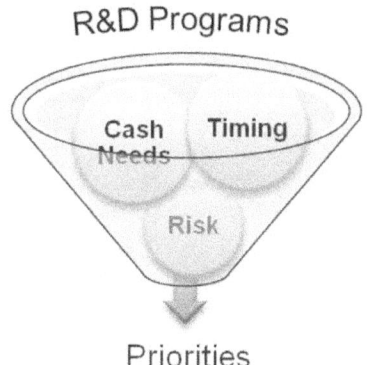

FIGURE 3–2: PRIORITIZING R&D PROGRAMS

In other words, programs requiring less cash investment, having lower risk, and generating returns (profit) in the near term become more attractive than high–risk, high–reward, longer–term programs that require greater cash investment.

To illustrate program evaluation and then prioritization based on these three factors, we provide examples of two easy–to–use methodologies.

EXAMPLE 1: TIMING AND CASH NEEDS

Figure 3–3 below shows one way to compare the value of potential programs as measured by the combination of time to profit and profit itself. In this plot, we are using negative profit as a measure of the cash needs (investment), and positive profit as a measure of the probable future cash generated. Keeping in mind the goal (minimizing cash investment in the short term without jeopardizing the future), which program is best?

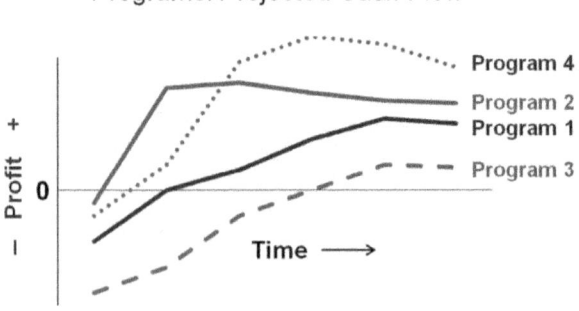

FIGURE 3–3: TIME VERSUS PROFIT
(INVESTMENT REQUIRED OR CASH GENERATED)

The first answer is not Program 3, where it looks like it will take a very long time and a large amount of cash to achieve profitability. And in this case, the profits never offset the cash investment. Program 1 looks better than Program 3, but it probably is not the first choice either. It offers no advantages (based on cash required, time–to–profit, and probable amount of profit) over programs 2 and 4.

Therefore, Programs 2 and 4 look best. Program 4 requires little cash and provides the highest yearly profits in a reasonable timeframe. And Program 2 also needs minimal cash and shows profits that are reasonable and sustainable. In addition, the time to positive profit for Program 2 is the shortest.

This example shows a useful way to compare programs and establish preliminary priorities. However, this kind of analysis, by itself, isn't enough information to make final decisions. At the very least, risk also should be considered, as the next example shows.

EXAMPLE 2: RISK VERSUS REWARD

One way to put program risk in perspective is to consider risk versus expected returns (reward). For this example, returns mean profits. However, you could use other measures such as market share. Risk includes factors such as business fit, competitive advantage, proprietary position, technical feasibility, and ability to leverage core competencies. These elements, taken together, determine a program's overall risk—its "probability of success". You can determine a program's probability of success subjectively or with a "scorecard" approach (38).

Whatever approach you use, once you have determined the expected returns and probabilities of success for each program, there are various ways that you can compare and prioritize them.

Figure 3–4 below illustrates one simple way of doing this. Here we have plotted each program's expected return or reward (at some determined point in time) versus its probability of success (reciprocal of Risk).

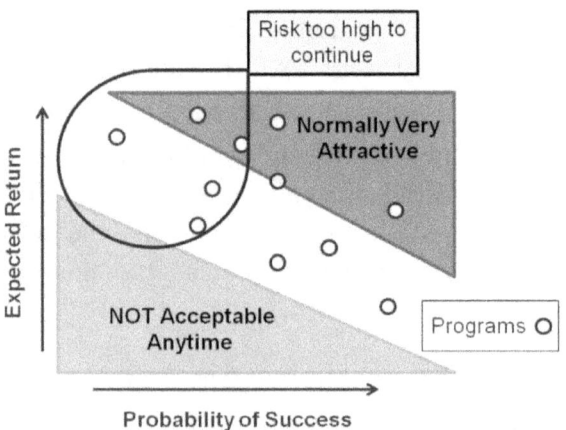

R&D Program Assessment

FIGURE 3–4: PROGRAM REWARD (RETURN) VERSUS DECREASING RISK (PROBABILITY OF SUCCESS)

As is shown, if the expected return and the probability of success are both high, the program fits in the dark gray triangle area—very attractive. In normal economic times, these all would be the higher priority programs and candidates for increased resources. Conversely, if the risk is high (probability of success is low) and the expected returns are low, the program falls into the light gray area—not acceptable. These are programs that are candidates for cost/resource cutting at all times unless there is some compelling reason for keeping them. And then there are the programs that fit "in–between" and may need additional assessment.

However, the situation changes somewhat in difficult economic times. Businesses in crisis usually cannot afford to take the same level of risk that they were comfortable with in good times. Therefore those programs that are higher risk, even though they offer potentially high returns, are less attractive—the area in *Figure 3–4* that is circled and labeled "risk too high to continue."

These two examples illustrate simple techniques you can use to assist in prioritizing programs. However, your specific business situation, other measures of program value (e.g., strategic importance), and the effect on your organization all are factors that need to be considered before taking action. And there are many other approaches to program prioritization that you can discover with a little internet searching (key words like "product portfolio"). Reference (37) also can be a good resource.

But, as is the case in most areas of business decision–making in disruptive times, there are no rigid rules for prioritizing R&D programs. However we offer some general guidelines:

- Pick your prioritization criteria based on your business specifics
- Focus on *time* to returns (not just returns)
- Be more *risk averse*
- Consider the magnitude of the *immediate* investment required
- Don't forget your *future* (Strategic Importance)

R&D Resource Changes

Once you have established R&D program priorities, then your challenge becomes using those priorities to make appropriate funding/spending decisions relating to R&D. Basically this is a two part process.

First, reduce R&D spending by cutting the least attractive programs (you decide the criteria based on your business situation). To be effective, this may involve some degree of downsizing. Then focus the remaining resources (cash and human resources) on the most important programs (those providing immediate cash flow benefits and/or preserving your future).

To help making your final decisions, here are some "checking" questions for you to consider:

- Even in good times would the program be a good one? Should it be cut no matter what?
- How essential is the program to your business recovery as the downturn eases?
- Can the program be delayed without causing irreversible harm?
- What about the human resources involved in the programs you decide to cut? Will you lose them, and can you afford that?

One plea. Resist the temptation for across–the–board R&D spending cuts. This approach seldom provides the benefits anticipated and often produces a long–lasting negative effect. Instead, keep in mind the goal: minimizing short–term cash investment without killing the possibility of future business growth.

BASIC SURVIVAL ADVICE

If possible, avoid survival tactics that will kill your organization's capability for innovation.

Increasing organizational productivity (downsizing and beyond), business rationalization (products, markets, and more), business model revision, and R&D spending optimization. All of these types of actions that we have explored in this chapter are a part of good business management at any time. And as we have shown, tactics focusing on these areas also provide numerous near–term opportunities for business survival and stabilization in challenging economic times.

However, as we have cautioned, actions such as these can have significant impact on the future health of a business. Therefore we end this chapter with one basic piece of advice: If at all possible, avoid implementing survival tactics that will kill your organization's capability for innovation thereby destroying your business future.

Innovation, and ultimately new products, are important even in difficult times. Just think about Amazon and the Kindle or Apple and the iPad or even Facebook. Need more convincing? Want more examples? See the articles in Reference (39).

Chapter 4

Turnaround Strategies

T he good news? Your business has survived the
worst of the crisis and achieved some level of
stability (at least temporarily). So what is next? Now is
the time to consider turnaround strategies—those
strategies that generally are focused on business
strengthening and longer–term growth. But what
turnaround strategies can or should you consider? That
is the subject of this chapter.

However, before exploring specific turnaround
strategies, it's important to take a step back and look
at the big picture of the "game" of business. This
provides the foundation on which to build "game–
changing" strategies and actions for the future.

THE BUSINESS "GAME"

> *"The essence of business success lies in making*
> *sure you're playing the right game." (40)*

Business can be viewed as a competitive, high–stakes
game. Just like any game, it has players and rules,
winners and losers. However the game of business is

not just about winning or losing or even how well you play. It's more complex than that:

> "Companies can succeed spectacularly without requiring others to fail. And they can fail miserably no matter how well they play if they make the mistake of playing the wrong game. The essence of business success lies in making sure you're playing the right game." (40)

But what is the "right" business game? To answer that question we start by exploring the basic framework of a business game—the players and the forces that drive an industry.

The Business Game Framework

Porter's 5 Forces Model for industry analysis (41) is the classic way to look at an industry's players and its dynamics—the framework of the business game. *Figure 4–1* is a simplified diagram that captures the key concepts of his model and expands on it slightly.

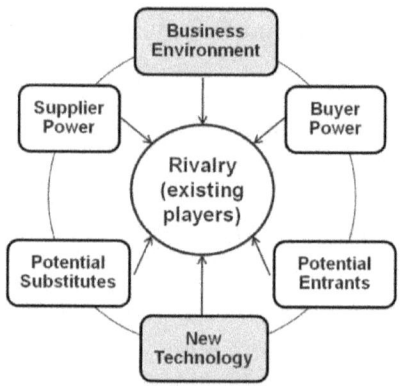

FIGURE 4–1: PORTER'S COMPETITIVE FORCES (42)

Although this picture implicitly includes the players, it focuses explicitly on the forces driving competition—those that create rivalry in the "game" of business. To elaborate on Figure 4·1, the competitive forces include:

- Rivalry among existing players (you and your competitors)

- The threat of new entrants or players (potential competitors, direct or indirect)

- The bargaining power of buyers (customers)

- The bargaining power of suppliers

- The threat of substitute products (usually those with lower cost or from another industry)

- The impact of new technology

- Other external forces in the business environment (regulatory, political, economic)

As the figure shows, all of these elements are interconnected. They influence each other and impact the business. Note: Porter's original "5 Forces" model does NOT include either New Technology or Business Environment directly. Strictly speaking, these can be considered as included in the other forces. However, due to their major impacts on industries and businesses in today's dynamic times, we have included them in our view of the "business game". For additional information on the interactions among Porter's basic competitive forces see Reference (41).

Once you understand the basic competitive framework for your specific business situation, your challenge is to determine what you can change in your business game to affect and/or use these forces in ways that create enough competitive advantage to turnaround your business and to provide opportunities for future growth. These are what we call Game Changing Actions.

Game-Changing Actions

As a starting point for developing specific game–changing actions, it's useful to consider Porter's three generic types of strategies for combating an industry's competitive forces (42). To summarize, competitive advantage can be created by:

1. *COST LEADERSHIP* (having lower costs than your competitors)

2. *DIFFERENTIATION* (offering or doing something that is considered unique or providing higher value)

3. *FOCUS* (channeling business efforts toward a specific target customer, market, or product)

Consider first *COST LEADERSHIP* strategies. These types of strategies could involve automation or outsourcing or selling through distribution or any number of other changes to your business framework (business model) that allow you to achieve a lower cost position than your competitors. The advantages of being the "low cost producer" are obvious and include things such as higher returns, more flexibility in pricing, and the ability to offer additional services and benefits to customers.

Next, think of *DIFFERENTIATION* strategies. Although creating new products is the most obvious example of this type of strategy, an innovative business model or a disruptive business practice can also can be effective in providing competitive advantage through differentiation (e.g., being the first to sell books on the internet with no physical store). Or, differentiation could mean adding value by providing higher product quality or better service or by increasing the value of existing products through product modification.

And third, there are *FOCUS* strategies— narrower, broader, or just different. First, think about narrowing the focus of a business to a specific geography or market segment or type of customer where the business has key strengths. This type of focus strategy often allows for more efficient and/or effective service to the particular target. In other words, a narrower focus results in a stronger presence in a more restricted business arena (i.e., a smaller but stronger business). But a focus strategy can also mean changing and/or broadening focus in order to address new and better business opportunities. This type of focus strategy can lead to turnaround and significant growth if executed properly.

Now, using the concepts embodied in these three generic strategies, what are some of the game–changing actions for creating competitive advantage? They fall into categories such as:

- Changing the Players
- Changing your Added Values
- Changing the Rules
- Changing the Geography
- Changing the Technology
- Expanding your Business Area

To learn more these types of game–changing actions see *"The Right Game: Use Game Theory to Shape Strategy"* by A. Brandenburger and B. Nalebuff (40). This is an understandable article that starts from a modification of Porter's 5 Forces model and explores the categories of actions highlighted above. For more detail, we recommend the book "CO–OPETITION" by the same authors (43).

But what kinds of changes should you consider in uncertain times? What strategies should you investigate as ways to strengthen your business and position it for the future, even in the midst of an economic downturn? Before addressing those questions directly, we provide an example that illustrates how a combination of game–changing actions can provide business turnaround in a challenging economy.

TURNAROUND THROUGH GAME–CHANGING ACTIONS

The Emerald Corporation sells proprietary (patented) two–way radios for use in luxury yachts. It sources semi–conductors from Japan, but all other components and the finished products are manufactured internally with semi–automated equipment.

Emerald was a highly successful, focused business before the economy changed. However, as the downturn intensified, a crisis developed. The company's revenues declined, manufacturing costs increased, and profits fell. The company quickly discovered that lowering prices had little effect on sales. Cash flow became a significant issue.

As we have stated previously, Emerald's situation (or something similar) is one that companies commonly find themselves facing at the onset of an economic downturn, with two exceptions. First, Emerald has no competitor that is lowering prices. In other words, Emerald has a unique product (and a very powerful brand name). Second, the price sensitivity for Emerald's products is low and has not changed. Thus, although the luxury market addressed by Emerald has decreased in size due to recession, lowering prices will not increase demand.

What should the Emerald Corporation do? The company's Executive Committee developed a multi–pronged turnaround strategy with five key elements:

1. Given their success with outsourcing semi–conductors, Emerald decided to purchase finished molded parts from a low–cost producer instead of manufacturing them internally (additional outsourcing to lower costs). The challenge: finding the right source quickly.

2. To increase production volumes and thus control costs, avoid massive layoffs and those with long–term consequences, and increase revenues; Emerald decided to sell their unique, high–end radios for other applications. The company determined that small aircraft, taxis and limousines offered significant potential, if prices were decreased. The challenges: quickly and cost effectively establishing distribution and sales capabilities to address these new segments and customers, and making sure that the additional revenues actually provide financial benefit (e.g., increased profit).

3. Emerald also decided to offer contract manufacturing services for other electronic products in order to gain revenues from their not–fully–utilized manufacturing equipment and capabilities, and thus reduce their own manufacturing costs through increased productivity. The challenges: finding customers, scaling–up the different products, providing cost–acceptable manufacturing.

4. Emerald attempted to increase their revenues by using their existing sales network to sell other companies' products for luxury yachts. They had determined this was possible without significant investment and thus should provide increased cash flow. The challenge: establishing suitable alliances.

5. Emerald decided to offer repair service (a highly profitable *NEW* business with minimal fixed costs) for their radios rather than contracting that service out to a third party. The challenge: establishing a cost effective customer service function.

Cost savings, productivity improvements, business model changes, new customers, new products, new businesses, alliances. Changing the players, changing the rules, changing the added value, and expanding the business area. Emerald has developed a comprehensive, multi–pronged strategy for business turnaround that incorporates all of these different types of game–changing actions.

However, the challenges Emerald will face are significant: the time it takes for effective implementation, the actual start–up costs, the real financial benefits provided. And since the turnaround plan requires developing new capabilities and/or finding suitable partners and/or making a significant cash outlay, the obstacles may be insurmountable if everything is attempted at once.

Therefore, although business turnaround usually requires a combination of strategies (such as those that Emerald planned), in the remainder of this chapter we address different "game–changing" actions individually. And we are selective. We focus on the specific types of "expansion" strategies that we believe are the most appropriate for business turnaround and positioning for growth in challenging economic times. These are:

- Finding new Markets for EXISTING Products
- Offering New/Modified Products
- Embracing New Businesses
- Using Alliances and Acquisitions

NEW MARKETS FOR EXISTING PRODUCTS

Be realistic. Don't overreach your capabilities and financial situation.

Finding new markets for existing products is an example of Porter's generic *"focus"* competitive strategy. But unlike business rationalization where the focus is narrowed, in this case the focus is broader. The specific game–changing actions we focus on are expanding your business to new geographies and/or finding new customers for your products. However it is important to keep in mind that both of these types of actions are likely to bring new players (competitors) into your business game.

New Geographies

First, consider the turnaround strategy of expanding a core business (existing products) to new geographic areas. This expansion can range from local to state–wide to national to international. Why can this type of strategy be so important? If your business is still recovering from a crisis situation, there usually is not enough time to develop completely new products. However, expanding sales of your *EXISTING* products (or possibly slightly modified products) into new geographic segments often can be done quickly and, if managed properly, without significant investment. In addition, this type of expansion also provides opportunities to focus on geographies less impacted by economic downturns and/or areas with less competition.

An example of this type of strategy was the planned addition by 7–Eleven of 200 new outlets in 2009 (44). Why was this considered? In spite of the recession, the demand for the company's products had remained relatively strong. But more important, because of the recession, there was increased availability of desirable retail space at affordable prices. Therefore expanding to new geographies, even if these sites were only a few blocks away from existing stores became a viable turnaround/growth action.

While the 7–Eleven example makes expanding to new geographies sound simple, there are several important factors to consider before attempting this type of action. These include:

- Competitors (existing and new) and their likely reactions to your moves
- How to expand your sales/distribution network
- Logistics/organizational issues
- Cost of expansion
- Ability to move rapidly enough
- Availability of partners, if needed
- Fit with your Core Competencies

The basic advice: Capitalize on your business core competencies and seek partners whose core competencies are different and provide synergy with yours when appropriate. But overall, be realistic. Don't overreach your capabilities and financial situation, and don't underestimate entrenched competition.

New Customers

Next, consider opportunities for business expansion through new types of customers for your *EXISTING* products. This is exactly what Emerald did when they identified small aircraft, taxis, and limousines as potential target markets for their radios.

If you can do the same and identify new market segments and/or new applications/uses for your existing products, you have a good opportunity for business turnaround and even expansion. And in this case (versus business expansion into new geographies) you may have a better chance to focus on markets less impacted by an economic downturn.

As an example of this type of game–changing strategy, consider the actions by Starbucks in 2010 (45). In a counter–attack against lower–priced rivals, the coffee giant rolled out a second coffee brand (Seattle's Best) to super markets, convenience stores, fast–food outlets, and even vending machines. In addition, they added their Via coffees and Tazo teas to the mix. And they were successful in expanding their business through these new types of customers.

However, before you jump into this type of game–changing action, remember that a key challenge is focusing on the *best* new customers, not just any new customer. Picking the wrong customers can rapidly worsen your business financial situation.

In addition, it's still important to consider the same factors that we listed in the previous section. It's also important to keep in mind that business expansion through new customers may be a bigger step than expansion through new geographies since you probably will be entering types of markets where you currently have no experience. In this situation, developing an understanding of new competitors and determining customer service requirements are critical issues. In addition, some sort of partnership or other business alliance is more likely to be required in order to be successful.

Then, like with any game–changing strategy, once you have chosen your customer focus, the challenge becomes implementation.

NEW PRODUCTS AND SERVICES

*Turnaround through innovation and
acting "outside of the box"*

Offering new products and/or services generally fits Porter's generic *"differentiation"* strategy category. This type of strategy can involve several game changing actions such as changing your added values, changing the technology, and even changing the rules of your particular business game. Keeping the objective of business turnaround in mind, we explore this type of strategy from two different perspectives: new products/services that are the result of your own efforts (internal focus) and others' products/services that could be available to you (external focus).

Internal Focus

First consider your own *NEW* products. Can you improve your business financials from *NEW PRODUCTS* that you already are in the process of developing? More specifically, are there any *internal* new product development programs that could be accelerated to provide relatively short–term financial benefit, leading to business turnaround and growth?

What do we mean by "programs that could be accelerated" or more broadly *"program acceleration"*? Often a number of different new product development programs are being carried out at the same time, each with different timelines and priorities. Consider the possibility of focusing resources on specific programs sequentially instead of concurrently, with the highest priority being given to the new product program closest to commercialization. If such focus shortens the time–to–market, we call this program acceleration.

There are several important criteria for identifying new product programs that are good acceleration candidates. These include programs that:

- Are almost ready for commercialization
- Require limited additional investment
- Offer potential for short–term positive cash flow
- Address market segments less affected by the recession
- Can be significantly expedited with increased focus and/or resources

Following are two examples of ways to use some of these criteria to compare different programs. You may find these or similar techniques useful in making your choices.

First we take a look at the effect that increasing investment has on the time–to–market by "plotting" the investment required to accelerate/complete a new product program versus the decrease in time–to–market which that investment would provide. This approach is illustrated in *Figure 4–2* on the next page.

In this case, a qualitative approach often is good enough to give a picture of the cost/effect balance of acceleration and to answer questions such as: How costly is the program, including acceleration costs? Does the potential change in time to market justify the costs? Can your business afford the level of investment, even if the acceleration effects are great?

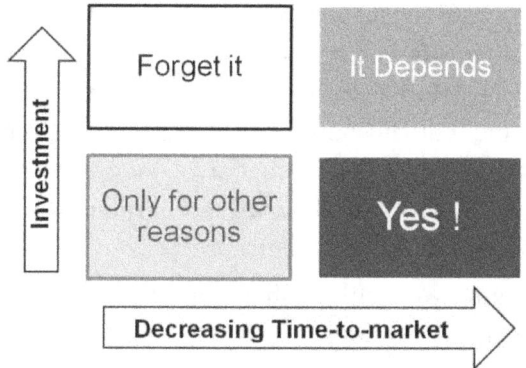

FIGURE 4–2: COST EFFECTIVENESS OF ACCELERATION

Specifically, plotted on the vertical axis is the investment needed to accelerate the commercialization of a new product program. On the horizontal axis, the effect of that investment is plotted, as measured by decreasing time–to–market (the larger the decrease in the time to market, the greater the acceleration). Then the results are divided into four boxes.

Programs falling in the upper left–hand box require high investment with little change in time–to–market (not acceptable candidates for acceleration). The lower left–hand box represents the case where only a small additional investment is needed to accelerate/complete a program, but not much acceleration results from the investment. Programs falling in that box also are not good candidates for acceleration, but the cost of completing the program (commercializing the new product) is low, so there may be other reasons to make/continue the investment.

Programs falling in the lower right–hand box are the best candidates for acceleration focus since they can be significantly accelerated at low cost. However, if you can afford it, programs falling in the top right–hand box (significant investment required) also may be good acceleration candidates (significant decrease in time to market possible). In both cases, additional information such as risk involved and expected contributions to cash flow after commercialization is needed to make the best choices.

Figure 4–3 below shows a way to compare one of the additional factors—cash.

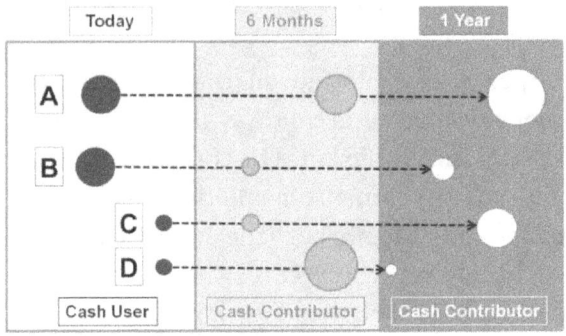

FIGURE 4–3: ACCELERATION AND CASH FLOW

This example assumes that you have identified several possible internal candidate programs for acceleration (A, B, C, D) and focuses on cash and cash flow.

Today (the left box), all of these programs are cash users (black bubbles), with the sizes of the black bubbles representing relative amounts of cash required to complete each program. All four programs can be accelerated and become cash contributors in 6 months, as is shown in the middle box (gray bubbles). Again, for the 6 month period, the sizes of the bubbles represent the relative amounts of cash generated.

You could stop at this point and make your choices. However, even in unsettled times, six months is a very short period. We recommend also looking at a one–year projection (shown in the box on the right). In our example, all programs are still cash contributors in this time frame, with the sizes of the white bubbles representing the relative amounts of cash generated.

So which program is the best choice for acceleration focus? Not program B. It is expensive to accelerate/complete and the amount of cash generated is small both in the 6–month and the 1–year timeframe. If you look only at the 6 month timeframe, you would choose program D since it requires little investment to complete and generates the largest amount of cash. But the situation is very different if you look at the 1–year cash contributions. However, if you have little cash and an urgent need for more, program D still might the right choice. Or, if you can afford it, accelerating both Program A and Program C could be a good strategy.

As you can see, the final choice is not always simple. What is best depends on your specific business situation. For more information on program evaluation and methodologies for accelerating new product programs, we recommend the books: "WINNING AT NEW PRODUCTS: ACCELERATING THE PROCESS FROM IDEA TO LAUNCH" by R. Cooper (46a) and "DEVELOPING PRODUCTS IN HALF THE TIME" by P. Smith and D. Reinertsen (46b).

But perhaps you do not have any new product programs that are good choices to accelerate. Then, you might want to consider new products from external sources—the next game changing strategy we explore for business turnaround.

External Focus

There are several ways your business can benefit from new products from *external* sources (others' products). The most obvious of these is to obtain new products for your business through acquisition, partnership, or some other sort of business arrangement.

However there are other possibilities. For example, you could sell others' products using your sales/distribution network and/or you could make products for others using your manufacturing capability. In both of these cases, your own "new products" are services (contract sales, contract manufacturing). However, since these services are focused on products that "belong" to others, we view these new services as belonging to the external new product category. As you might recall from our earlier example, the Emerald Corporation combined several of these types of actions in its turnaround plan.

But don't ignore more innovative solutions. For example, consider the growing practice within the retail industry of "stores within stores". The idea is to provide floor space within one store to another company's brand and products. This can take various forms such as those described in the article *"Ten Retailers Turning Department Stores into Mini–Malls"* and includes various benefits:

> *"For the brands, they're immediately getting— overnight almost—hundreds of locations for very low capital investment ... and of course,*

the department stores are gaining a whole other consumer market and/or a whole new product category." (47)

Although using external products in ways such as those we have highlighted above often appears attractive for business financial improvement, this turnaround strategy usually has higher risk than one that focuses on internal new products – unless the external products are *CLOSELY RELATED* to your current products or are synergistic with your current business. In addition, some of the approaches we have highlighted are likely to force you to revise your business model.

Therefore, before acting, it is essential to take into account your current business situation and capabilities. In this assessment, it is important to be realistic and to thoroughly evaluate the financials (costs and benefits) of acquiring, selling, and/or manufacturing the specific *"external"* new products and services under consideration. And it is critical to identify any gaps in needed core competencies and to determine how to cope with them. We strongly recommend involving the appropriate functional experts in these assessments (e.g., Controller, R&D and Manufacturing leaders, etc.).

NEW BUSINESSES

A path that dramatically alters your business game.

Now a bigger step—*turnaround through new businesses*, not just new products. If you can quickly develop/acquire businesses in markets healthier than your current ones (more resistant to economic downturns) or with different cost structures (e.g. low fixed costs assuming that yours are high) or where your core competencies (or your new partner's) provide you with unique capabilities and advantages, you can dramatically alter your business game. If successful, you will have created a path toward improved financial health for your business.

However, this path is not always an easy one to follow. The obvious prerequisites are cash and resource availability. It also is probable that you will need to define your business differently (expand/change your "Business Definition") to allow you to move into areas outside of your core businesses (high risk). Additionally, in order to act quickly, you are likely to need an alliance or acquisition. But the benefits can be great—ranging from capturing market share in more attractive business segments to opening up new and larger business opportunities.

So, assuming that your company is in a position to pursue a new business, how do you determine what new business to develop or acquire? That depends on your current *"Business Definition"* and how you choose to change or expand it—the topics of the next two sections.

Your Current Business Definition

Unlike your Business Model that defines how you carry out your business, your *Business Definition* answers the question: Who are you? This is the most basic question about your business. To be more specific, a

Business Definition (sometime called "mission") answers questions such as:

- What Business are you in? Who are your customers? What need do you address, and how do you meet that need?
- What products do you provide to what markets?
- What is the scope of your business (Industries and Market Segments, Geographies)?

Looking at it from a different perspective, a business definition can be conceptual or based on technologies, products, customers or markets. A *conceptual* business definition describes what your business hopes to become and how. A *technology–based* business definition stresses your technology core competencies. A *product–based* business definition focuses on the products or services you offer while a *customer–based* business definition focuses on the kinds of people or businesses you serve and the needs they have. A *market–based* business definition defines your business in terms of your current market segments, including geographic distribution.

Whatever approach you take, your Business Definition does not need to be lengthy, but it should be clear. It can be very simple: "My Company will provide Product X to Market Y." However some detail is more useful: "My Company is a high quality, contract manufacturer of electronic devices for the health care industry." Or: "My Company designs and sells innovative products to help generate a healthy indoor climate for commercial office buildings." For a more detailed look at the concept of "Business Definition" and its importance see References (48), (49), and (50).

As is apparent from the above simple examples, your Business Definition defines both business constraints and business scope. And, whether or not you explicitly consider it, *your Business Definition dictates many of your strategic actions.* In other words, your choice of new business opportunities to pursue is likely to be limited by your current Business Definition. So, to achieve turnaround through new businesses, it often is necessary to expand your Business Definition.

Expanding You Business Definition

The premise: Expanding your Business Definition (defining your business differently) broadens the possibilities for game–changing strategies that can lead to significantly improved business performance through new businesses. However there is no guarantee of success. The way you choose to expand your Business Definition is key. We highlight three important factors to consider.

The first factor is the TYPE of business. For various reasons (environmental, political, etc.) some business areas may be considered unacceptable. The reasons these are "forbidden" don't matter, but they are off–limits. Only businesses supported by "management" can be considered as expansion areas.

Next, consider the FINANCIALS. Here the intensity of competition and the general financial characteristics of the particular business area (e.g., typical profits, growth, etc.) are important to consider. Only business areas where acceptable financial results are probable should be considered for expansion.

Now, think about RISK. To have a reasonable probability of success in a new business area, it is best that it be somewhat associated with your existing business. Trying to achieve business goals in unfamiliar territory where core competencies cannot be relied on, leads to frequent failure. In addition, different organizations have different risk tolerances. You must understand yours and judge new business areas accordingly. Only those businesses judged to present acceptable risk should be considered as expansion areas. This narrows the possibilities even further.

The resulting overlap of the "business areas" identified by combining the above three factors (acceptable type, financials, and risk) defines the business arena to consider when expanding your business definition.

Figure 4–4 below illustrates graphically a process to do what we have just described in words.

FIGURE 4–4: EXPANDING YOUR BUSINESS DEFINITION

Starting with all businesses (the largest white oval), first identify those kinds of businesses that are of an acceptable type—represented by the somewhat smaller marble textured oval within the space of all businesses. Then, considering that subset, determine which of those businesses have acceptable financials—represented by the even smaller white oval. Finally, from that smaller subset of businesses that are both of an acceptable type and have acceptable financials, identify those that also have acceptable risk. The gray oval represents that more restricted business world.

Presumably your current business (represented by the small, black oval) falls within that gray circle. Therefore the part of the gray oval that is outside of your current business oval, defines the acceptable expansion area for your business. In other words, businesses which fall in the gray oval are viable new business candidates. They are acceptable in type, offer attractive financial prospects, involve risk that is within your "comfort zone", and have not yet been exploited by you.

There are numerous examples of companies that have expanded their business definitions to pursue new businesses. Two companies that illustrate different approaches to doing this in order to capture new business opportunities are Dell and Amazon.

Dell chose to make numerous acquisitions to reduce its dependence on PC's. This has allowed them to enter somewhat related new businesses such as smart–phones, computer storage, and services (51).

Amazon, on the other hand, has used multiple e–commerce innovations to provide new business opportunities. Just think about it. Once, not very long ago, Amazon was only an online bookstore. Now it is *THE* mega general retailer of the Web (52).

These examples illustrate clearly the actions of two companies with two different turnaround strategies, placing their bets on growth through expanded business definitions and new business opportunities.

OK, let's assume you are convinced that expanding your Business Definition to include a broader but still acceptable business arena is the first step in turnaround through new businesses. The next challenge is to identify the best new business opportunities within that expanded arena.

The Best New Business Opportunities

Maybe you are considering developing new businesses yourself such as Amazon did. Or perhaps you are taking Dell's approach and considering acquisitions. In either case, it's important to compare the potential risks and rewards related to your specific candidates.

Figure 4–5 on the next page shows one way to do this based on a risk/reward methodology championed by 3M in the 1980's (53). Although this is a qualitative approach, it can provide useful guidance. Specifically, increasing "reward" or expected return (sales, profits, cash flow) is plotted on the vertical axis. Decreasing risk, represented by increasing relationship to your current business and/or core competencies, is plotted on the horizontal axis (the more related, the lower the risk).

Relationship to Current Business

FIGURE 4-5: ASSESSING BUSINESS RISK VERSUS REWARD

The "DOG" box defines an area of low return and high risk (unrelated to your current business and/or capabilities). New Businesses falling in this area are generally poor candidates for providing turnaround in difficult economic times (or even in good times). However, if you can afford it, there may be strategic reasons for considering *acquiring* (not developing) these types of businesses (strategic markets, needed technology or other competencies, etc.).

The "STAR" box is the opposite of the "dog". It defines the area of new businesses with high returns and low risk (businesses closely related to yours and/or a good fit with your core competencies). New businesses fitting in this box offer excellent possibilities for turnaround and growth. If these types of businesses can be acquired, that's one approach. But often, internal development is a possibility. However, if you follow this path, it is important to keep in mind that the probability of being successful may be increased through strategic "partnerships".

Just think about Apple and the iPhone. This new business was a good choice for Apple based on the combination of its existing products, capabilities and services: state–of–the–art PC's, touch–screen technology, design, iTunes and apps, and the Apple store. But these factors wouldn't have been enough. By adding an alliance with AT&T (then called Cingular) to these building blocks, Apple's iPhone became a best–selling phenomenon (54).

The "HELP" box is just that. New businesses falling there offer high return but are high risk (unrelated to your business). They may be acceptable turnaround candidates if you can find a suitable partner or acquisition. However this kind of diversification often can be a distraction leading to disaster. As an example, consider RCA (now defunct, but once a powerful electronics company). In the difficult economic times of the 1970s, RCA acquired Hertz (rental cars), Banquet (frozen foods), Coronet (carpeting), Random House (publishing) and Gibson (greeting cards). All of these were "healthy" companies, however they were unrelated to RCA's core businesses and to each other. Thus each required significant management attention, at the expense of RCA's core businesses, causing serious financial problems (55).

The "BAND–AID" box defines the area where returns are low, but the risk is also low (closely related to your business). Although these businesses are not necessarily good turnaround candidates, they may have short–term value for business stabilization and could offer some strategic advantages.

Of course, there are critical success factors other than risk and reward to consider when evaluating new business opportunities such as timing and investment required. Unless you can afford it and the new business produces positive financial results in your needed timeframe, it won't help fuel your business turnaround and/or provide growth.

ALLIANCES AND ACQUISITIONS

Creative business "partnerships" can be extremely important in difficult economic times.

New markets, new products and services, and new businesses. Whatever you choose for your game–changing turnaround strategy, it's important to consider possible alliances, mergers, acquisitions, and other creative business arrangements to strengthen your position. Such relationships can provide key advantages both in carrying out short–term survival tactics such as discussed in Chapter 3 and in implementing the turnaround strategies we have explored in this Chapter. To summarize, these advantages include:

- Quicker access to new markets (geographies and customers) and new products
- More rapid and successful expansion into new business areas
- Increased organizational productivity and business efficiency
- New capabilities to augment your core competencies

And, there are other reasons for establishing new relationships during difficult economic times. For example, acquisitions often can be made at a lower price, and companies generally are more open to different kinds of alliances and business arrangements. Of course, to establish a meaningful new business relationship, the financial situation of your company must be such that it can afford an acquisition or is considered attractive as a partner. Or alternatively, your company must offer some other unique and desirable capability or advantage. In addition, for a new relationship to be successful in providing turnaround performance in an appropriate timeframe, synergy is key. Some of the common kinds of synergies to look for in a "partner" include manufacturing equipment, customers, distribution, technology, and other core competencies.

By synergy in each of these areas we mean that your capabilities and those of your "partner" fill the gaps in each other's *core competencies* and/or create new and stronger capabilities than either or you have alone. Thus the right kinds of synergy from the right new relationship can help with cash conservation and productivity and can expedite your financial turnaround. Conversely, if there is no synergy in a relationship, the probability of it being a productive one is low as the RCA example described in the previous section illustrates (55).

The subject of acquisitions and alliances is complex, and it is not our intention to address this area in detail. There are many books available that provide in–depth information and analyses. For our purposes, it's enough to emphasize (and reiterate) that creative business "*partnerships*" can be extremely important in difficult economic times and should be considered as a part of any turnaround or growth strategy. However, if you are considering an alliance or acquisition, it's important to keep in mind the challenges involved in making such relationships successful. For perspectives on this, see Reference (56).

GENERAL GUIDELINES

> *"If you know where you want to go and how to get there, a recession is by far the best time to improve your relative strategic position." (57d)*

This chapter has been all about strategies for business turnaround in–the–midst–of or after a financial crisis. We have explored actions ranging from addressing new geographies and new customers to offering new products to finding and embracing new businesses. And we have touched on the importance of alliances and acquisitions for carrying out such actions.

Obviously, there isn't a single "silver bullet" that will turnaround a business. A combination of actions and relationships usually are necessary. Therefore we can't recommend a preferred path. However, there are some general guidelines that we offer to those developing turnaround strategies.

First of all, work from your STRENGTHS (core competencies). If your strength is Marketing/Sales, consider expansion to new customers and geographies, or even new businesses. If your strength is R&D, consider internally developed new products. If your strength is manufacturing, consider new business models.

Next, find a suitable partner or develop a new relationship if the opportunity is good but outside of your area of expertise and/or if timing requires it. And, if you have something unique to offer, seek opportunities for synergy with others.

Finally, before setting your course, carefully consider the benefits and risks involved by taking a close look at the financial impact of both success and failure. This should include accurately determining the investment needed and the timing required. Bottom line, make sure that you can afford your actions.

For additional insights on business turnaround, see the articles in Reference (57). The first article provides an excellent summary of how to combine many of the actions we have explored into a turnaround plan. The second article provides insights into business survival and turnaround based on studies of how several hundred Fortune 500 companies lived through slumps and recessions. The third article describes a combination of survival/turnaround actions that Best Buy took in late 2008. You can be the judge as to their effectiveness. The fourth article is more general and addresses the challenge of business turnaround in disruptive times.

PART THREE

Riding the Waves

It's All About Leadership

Chapter 5

Putting It All Together

Now that your initial moves have produced some level of stability for your business, it is time to focus on longer term business survival by putting together your strategies and subsequent actions to achieve that goal.

But before we continue, there is one basic question that we have not addressed: *What is business survival?* We've used the term frequently, but what exactly does it mean to you? Is it winning, and if so, how do you define winning? Or is it something else? The answer is not as clear–cut as winning or losing in sports. However there is one certainty. If your company goes out of business, you have lost. Short of that, as a business leader, it is essential for you to determine what you consider *"survival"* for your specific business.

Making this basic decision about "survival" is a prerequisite for making other strategic decisions and determining the kinds of actions necessary to achieve that survival. For example, if survival means weathering the economic storm with your business intact, that decision leads to different strategies and actions than if you decide to keep only a part of your current business alive and exit from the rest.

However, defining business survival is only the first leadership challenge. No matter what a leader decides survival means for his/her business, there seldom is just one path to follow that leads toward that end–goal. There are almost always alternatives to consider—multiple possible combinations of tactics and strategies that might provide the desired results. When survival is at stake, it's up to the leader to make the best choices and make those choices quickly.

But just making the best decisions and making them rapidly isn't enough. However business survival is defined and whatever tactics and strategies are chosen, there are still other leadership challenges— combining those tactics and strategies into cohesive action plans and effectively implementing those plans to move the business forward in the chosen direction.

And all of this means change. Thus the final, continuing challenge of a business leader is to make the change happen—now and again and again.

Decision–making, action plans, and making change happen. These are the key leadership challenges for business survival that are the focus for the remainder of this chapter.

DECISION–MAKING

Business survival and turnaround depend on
making the best decisions quickly.

In today's chaotic world, there is one important business leadership skill that is often ignored: the ability to make the best possible decisions RAPIDLY. How does a business leader accomplish this? We believe that such "dynamic" business decision–making requires science–based management methodologies and tools. What is the scientific method all about, and what quantitative methodologies can be useful for business oriented decision–making? This section provides a brief introduction for those wishing to consider using "science–based decision–making" as a leadership tool.

The Scientific Method

The *scientific method* is a logical, data–based approach to investigating phenomena and developing new knowledge. This method consists of the collection of data through observation and experimentation, followed by the formulation and testing of theories based on that data. If new experiments "validate" the theories (i.e., the theories predict the results of the new experiments), the theories then can be used to predict other future results.

The explosive advances in technology and science of the past 100 years have been made by applying this logical and quantitative method to what was once an empirical world. These large leaps forward were made when science started tackling problems that could not be solved by the empirical approach typical of the 19th century and earlier.

More recently (toward the end of the 20th century) it was shown that probabilistic theories using advanced computer–based technologies (initially in the field of military strategy) could be applied to problems that were previously thought to be inherently impervious to scientific methods, such as business management. Methodologies and tools based on such advances have the potential to change the business landscape irreversibly, but when?

In today's chaotic business environment, those businesses that are technically–oriented already have embraced some scientific methodologies in the operations arena (Research and Development, Engineering, Manufacturing, Finance, and to some extent Marketing). But many business leaders are still using empirical (or even intuitive) approaches for business planning and decision–making aimed at the future of the business. This is inadequate for making the best choices in a rapidly changing and highly competitive global environment. As is stated by Gary Hamel in his book "THE FUTURE OF MANAGEMENT" (58):

> "Management is out of date. Like the combustion engine, it's a technology that has largely stopped evolving, and that's not good."

But there is hope. There are management tools and methodologies that are being developed based on the principles of Game Theory and Agent Based Modeling and Simulation (ABMS) that will allow business leaders to apply quantitative techniques to the process of making business decisions rather than relying on intuition and experience. This will enable risk factors to be analyzed much more thoroughly in shorter time frames, leading to better and quicker decisions.   In other words, advances in business management science can help a company survive and grow when it finds itself in the path of a "Tsunami of Change" or, better yet, ride that wave to success.

However, it is not our intention to turn business leaders into specialists in using complex mathematical tools. Therefore, only brief overviews of different techniques are provided here. This is meant to increase awareness of their existence and to give enough information to facilitate making a choice as to which available methodologies and tools to use, *if the business situation warrants it.*

Science-based Decision-making

As we said earlier, in a disruptive environment such as today's, business survival, turnaround, and growth all depend on making the best decisions and making them quickly. If leaders use a logical process and have rapid access to the right information, they can anticipate the reactions of others and can proactively make rapid and better choices. This methodology, based on data, not intuition, is what we call *science–based decision–making.* It allows for rapid change and increases the chances for business success. In the next three parts of this section we highlight different computer–based methodologies that, to different degrees, inject science into the "art" of decision–making. For those not yet convinced of the value of a more scientific approach to leadership, we suggest that you look at one or more of the books in Reference (59).

These books are not textbooks or technical books, and they represent only a small selection of the writings about "philosophies" on what we are calling science–based decision–making. They all are easy to read and each offers a somewhat different perspective on decision–making in disruptive times. However, they all are proponents of injecting science into the art of decision–making and provide an excellent introduction to the somewhat more detailed information found in the remainder of this section. Now for the specifics.

BASIC COMPUTER MODELING

The various kinds of science–based decision–making methodologies and tools available can be divided into two categories: mostly qualitative and quantitative. In general, qualitative approaches are simpler to understand and use, but they provide only general guidance. In a normal business environment, these can be useful. However in an environment of disruptive change such as a post–recession world, more accurate data usually are needed to make the best decisions rapidly; and this requires a more quantitative approach.

The first (and simplest) quantitative approach to decision–making is basic computer modeling. This "spreadsheet" technique is used commonly by businesses today to analyze past financial results and to construct a future financial forecast mostly based on an extrapolation of the past results. Business Leaders then can use this information as the basis for their strategic and tactical decisions. This conventional approach is based on simple mathematical formulas and works fairly well in a *relatively stable* environment (calm economy, a steady and growing business, predictable competitors, no unexpected disruptions). In these circumstances, such basic tools may be adequate, and need no further description.

However, when disruptive changes occur, extrapolations of the future based on the past are no longer relevant. In other words, the past is no predictor of the future. *The "game" has changed and you don't know the "rules."* New methodologies and tools (such as described in the next two sections) are needed to predict quickly and more accurately possible future results. Although these mathematical simulation methodologies are more complex to implement than simple computer modeling, often requiring experts, they have the advantage that they can provide better predictions of outcomes for different scenarios. In other words, they can be used to more accurately explore the financial consequences of particular decisions for a variety of parameters and/or initial conditions.

GAME THEORY

Game Theory is an example of one powerful science–based approach that can more accurately evaluate alternative "futures." What is Game Theory? It is a branch of applied mathematics that is used in economics, biology, computer science and other disciplines. It attempts to mathematically model behavior and predict results in competitive situations, where the outcomes of an individual's choices depend on the choices of others. It was initially developed to analyze competitions where one individual does better at another's expense (the so–called "zero sum" game), but has been expanded to other competitive and/or cooperative situations.

This methodology, when applied to business, creates a "game" that consists of: a set of "players" (competitors), a set of "moves" (rational actions) available to those players, and a mathematical model that predicts the "payoffs" that the players might receive for each combination of actions. By "playing" this game, a leader can evaluate possible alternative outcomes of encounters with competing organizations that may have parallel and/or conflicting goals. In other words, Game Theory can help leaders make better strategic decisions in complex situations by predicting the probable consequences of the collective actions and reactions of the players.

The basic principles of Game Theory can be applied qualitatively to provide general guidance, but a full quantitative model may be needed to predict outcomes in the complex and dynamic economic environment of the post–recession world. The general characteristics of these two approaches (qualitative and quantitative) are summarized below in *Figure 5–1*.

GAME THEORY

Qualitative	Quantitative
Uses basic concepts to create simple models	Uses complex math to create sophisticated models
Non experts able to develop models and use them	Experts needed for model development and "game playing"
Provides rapid insight into options but only general guidance	Particularly useful when there are multiple players and options
Applies systematic thinking to business decisions	Requires time and a significant financial investment

FIGURE 5–1: QUALITATIVE VS. QUANTITATIVE GAME THEORY

First, consider what we call *Qualitative* Game Theory. This is a logical process that uses the basic concepts of Game Theory (but not the complex mathematics) to create simple models of competitive business situations. The model framework is developed by establishing the players, the goals, the possible actions (assumed to be rational), and the constraints (including timing). Sometimes just having this basic information is valuable. Then the game is "played" by answering logically "what if and then what" questions for a number of possible actions by the players.

Visualization of the game is helpful and is often accomplished by using a matrix approach or a "decision tree" diagram such as the one we illustrated in Chapter 2 (Pricing, *Figure 2–7*). For additional examples, see Reference (60). Usually this type of "game" will clearly identify some options that are undesirable and others that deserve further consideration. Therefore, although the guidance is general, qualitative Game Theory can be a useful decision–making methodology *when timing is critical and mathematical experts unavailable.*

On the other hand, *Quantitative* Game Theory is not simple. Developing accurate models requires the use of advanced mathematical tools that are not common knowledge among business leaders. Therefore leaders must find and rely on appropriate experts for model development and application (game playing). Even though this approach is complex, it can be worthwhile for a large company or a complicated business situation. It is particularly useful for exploring alternatives when there are multiple players, conflicting goals, and many action options. However, be cautious. The more complex your business situation, the more complex the mathematics are. In addition, Game Theory assumes that the players always make rational choices, and that doesn't always happen in the real world or business.

Bottom line, quantitative Game Theory can be a powerful tool, but it takes investment—in time and in people. The good news is that there are a number of consultants and experts available who have experience in successful business applications of this methodology. For additional information about both qualitative and quantitative Game Theory, see References (43), (60) and (61). You can also find additional articles and references through online research. One of the sites that you may find useful lists a number of consulting firms that specialize in Game Theory (62). Note: The authors do NOT have knowledge of any of these firms, and hence this reference in our book should in no way be considered a recommendation or an endorsement.

AGENT–BASED MODELING AND SIMULATION

Although Game Theory provides an excellent logical framework for simulating business situations, the complexity of the real business world makes the development of rigorous models difficult. The decision–making methodology highlighted in this section, *Agent–Based Modeling and Simulation* (ABMS), is a somewhat simpler science–based tool, at least in its application.

ABMS is a computer–enabled methodology that describes (and predicts) the evolution of dynamic systems by simulating the behavior of their constituent "agents" (individual parts or players). In other words, ABMS is a modeling technique that rapidly converts knowledge of a large number of individual behaviors into an understanding of overall system–level outcomes. To do this, it combines elements of Game Theory and complexity science, and uses Monte Carlo methods to introduce randomness. Below, *Figure 5–2* summarizes the key attributes of ABMS.

Agent-Based Modeling & Simulation (ABMS)

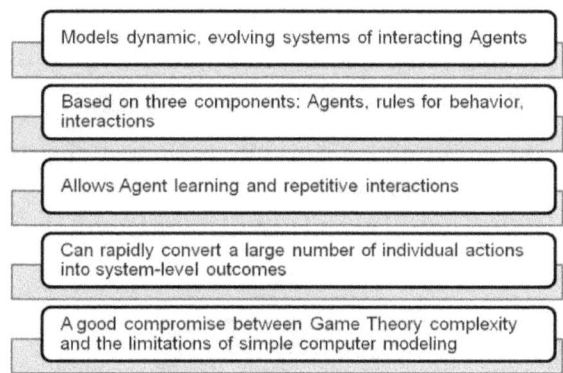

Models dynamic, evolving systems of interacting Agents

Based on three components: Agents, rules for behavior, interactions

Allows Agent learning and repetitive interactions

Can rapidly convert a large number of individual actions into system-level outcomes

A good compromise between Game Theory complexity and the limitations of simple computer modeling

FIGURE 5–2: KEY ATTRIBUTES OF ABMS

As mentioned above, with ABMS, a system (e.g., your market) is modeled as a collection of entities called Agents. More specifically, each Agent individually makes decisions and acts based on a set of rules appropriate for the system it represents (e.g., producing, selling, buying). ABMS can create thousands of individual Agents rapidly, and it allows "learning" and repetitive interactions among these Agents to occur. This enables the system to evolve and unanticipated behaviors to emerge (emergent phenomena). This adaptive feature allows ABMS to explore complex system dynamics which are out of the reach of the pure mathematics of Game Theory. In other words, ABMS has the ability to quickly calculate potential outcomes such as market shares, sales, and profitability and to provide strategic insights into future marketplace behavior.

Several key features differentiate ABMS from Game Theory. To summarize, ABMS:

- Builds the market (predicted outcomes) "bottom" up from many individual interactions.

- Uses data in many forms from many sources.

- Analyzes multiple scenarios rapidly.

- Does not require rational actions and allows for adaptive behavior.

- Can produce unanticipated emergent phenomena.

Thus, ABMS is an excellent science–based methodology to help leaders make decisions about problems with many interrelated but unpredictable elements. However, it is important to keep in mind that models, no matter how sophisticated, can only project probable outcomes, not actual reality. Therefore it is up to the decision–maker to use those projections wisely.

The books in Reference (63) provide good introductions to ABMS. Additionally, the Internet articles in Reference (64) provide general overviews of ABMS and/or actual examples of ABMS applied to business situations. The full texts of all of these articles are available online at no charge.

Reference (65) is an additional reference that you may find particularly interesting. This is a special issue of "*The Journal of Innovation Management*" which focuses on Agent–Based Modeling of innovations. In addition, a topic we have not dealt with is so–called "Participatory ABMS." This is a technique where human Agents are included in ABMS. Reference (66) describes this in more detail and discusses the potential advantages of this methodology.

We hope that this very brief introduction to "science–based decision–making" has convinced you of the value of this leadership approach in today's chaotic business environment. Although it doesn't guarantee "winning" in turbulent times, using a more quantitative and data–based methodology for decision–making will optimize your chances of successfully "riding" the Tsunami of change. In addition, Reference (67) describes different approaches to decision–making that you may find useful.

SURVIVAL ACTION PLAN

It's all about programs and priorities and defined actions for carrying out those programs.

So, you've made some key moves to stabilize your business—some internally focused for immediate damage control, others that are more defensive in nature (see Chapters 1 and 2). How long have those actions taken? Hopefully it has been just a few weeks, not several months. And, you've determined what the survival goal is for your business as well as made key decisions with respect to business survival tactics and turnaround strategies that support that goal.

Now on to the next leadership challenge: developing a comprehensive plan for turning those strategies and tactics into tangible results—results that optimize the probability of longer–term business

survival. This is what we call a *"Survival Action Plan."*
What is the timeframe to keep in mind for such a plan?
Six to eighteen months would be a good starting point.

In the remainder of this section we describe a
process for creating and documenting such a plan.
Note: a more detailed version of this process can be
found in Chapters 4 and 5 of our book "DYNAMIC
BUSINESS PLANNING BASICS" (2).

This process, like any planning process, is all
about programs and priorities and defined actions for
carrying out those programs. More specifically, this
process can be divided into four sequential steps:

1. Selecting and Prioritizing Programs
2. Developing Functional Plans to implement the
    chosen programs
3. Verifying Expected Outcomes and revising the
    plan if needed
4. Documenting the Plan

The results: a detailed set of integrated action plans
that can serve as your roadmap to business survival.
And the trip towards survival needs to start right now.
Exactly how long will that trip take? It is hard to say
because that depends both on your specific business
situation and on external forces beyond your control.

Programs and Priorities

Selecting specific programs to support your strategies
and establishing clear priorities among those programs
and other business survival tactics are the challenges
in this step. The techniques we introduced earlier to
evaluate programs (Chapter 3, R&D Program

Prioritization) can be used as a starting point, including the Real–Win–Worth analysis described in Reference (36).

However, although the programs being considered at this point might be R&D programs, they are just as likely to be "projects" associated with manufacturing, marketing, or supporting specific products. Therefore there are additional important factors (beyond those discussed in Chapter 3) that need to be assessed before making your choices. These factors can be divided into two categories: risk factors and factors relating to importance/value.

The factors relating to risk determine how likely it is that the program will be successful—its probability of success. Risk Factors include attributes such as business fit, product competiveness, match with your core competencies, investment required, and resource availability. And each of these attributes has important "sub–attributes." For example, product competiveness includes factors such as cost, performance, and proprietary position. And resource availability includes things such as cash, capital equipment, and human resources with the right skill sets and talents.

The factors relating to importance/value address the overall importance of a program and its worth to your business. These factors include things such as strategic importance, size of the opportunity, expected returns, and time to expected returns.

There are many different ways to assess program risk and importance/value such as those described in the previously referenced book "WINNING AT NEW PRODUCTS" by R. Cooper (46a). In addition there are many other ways that you can discover for yourself with a little Internet searching (keywords like "product portfolio").

What we haven't addressed directly are program priorities. What program is your business' top priority, what is next, and so on? *It is essential to establish clear program priorities and to communicate them to your organization.* Some of the same techniques used to select programs also can be used to prioritize them. However it is up to you to determine those that are best for your business and support the strategies that you have developed.

Whatever techniques you use to choose and prioritize your programs, it is important to be sure that the programs selected are consistent with your chosen strategies and your definition of business survival. In other words, you need to verify that you do indeed have appropriate programs defined to support each key strategy and that collectively those programs will allow you to achieve your survival goals.

Functional Plans

Once you have selected specific programs and established priorities, it's time for planning appropriate actions by each business Function (Marketing and Sales, Manufacturing, Research and Development, Quality, Engineering, etc.) related to those programs and priorities.. These functional plans have several important requirements.

First is consistency. The planned actions of each Function must be consistent with the survival goals, strategies, programs, and priorities for the overall business. In other words, it is important for there to be one agreed upon set of business priorities. Then, it is essential for each functional plan to be consistent with these. This means that each functional plan must support the implementation of the priority programs with resources, assigned responsibilities, and commitment to timelines and milestones.

But equally important is coordination and integration. To paraphrase what we stated in Chapter 3 relating to functional operations:

> *"No Function operates in isolation. Each is a critical element of the business, but each is dependent on all of the others. Therefore, for business survival it is essential that each Function's plans be integrated with the plans of the other Functions."*

In other words the programs and efforts of each individual Function must be coordinated with the programs and efforts of the other Functions. And each Function's actions must take into account the other Functions' constraints (skills, equipment, cash, etc.). This level of coordination and integration results in what we call "aligned functional plans."

Expected Outcomes

At this point, the survival planning process is almost complete. However, before documenting and implementing your plan, it is important to test your chosen course. What are the *COLLECTIVE* expected outcomes? Will the portfolio of priority programs that you have selected and planned achieve your survival goals if they are successful?

In other words, it's important to perform a gap analysis to determine if your proposed actions will take you to your desired arrival point (usually financial goals and other key business objectives), given your business constraints. More specifically, what are the overall projected results of your proposed survival plan? Are these results consistent with your survival goals, and is the investment exposure required to obtain these results acceptable?

A common way to assess expected financial outcomes of a proposed plan is to project sales and profits from the priority programs and then compare the combined results from all of these programs to the financial goals. We recommend that you do this.

However there are other considerations that are particularly important in times of financial difficulty. For example, it is critical to evaluate overall cash flow based on the timing and the collective amounts of required investments for the chosen portfolio of programs. This type of analysis is essential if there are only small reserves of cash or limited ability to borrow. In other words, it is important to determine if your proposed plan is financially acceptable and if you can afford to implement it.

Another important factor to consider for your proposed plan is the combined risk/reward balance. How risky is the new course? Do the potential rewards justify the risk? Can your business afford the level of risk? Here, as for the other criteria, it is important to consider the *TOTAL* portfolio—collective risks, sum of the investments required, and overall expected returns from your chosen priority programs.

Once you are satisfied that you understand the expected outcome from your proposed plan, you have reached the point in the planning process where you (the business leader) must decide whether or not to adopt the plan. If the expected outcome leads to the desired survival goals, within your business constraints (e.g., risk tolerance and availability of resources), accept the plan. But assuming that you do decide to go ahead, it is important to identify the critical issues and key success factors that will impact whether or not you are successful.

However, if the expected outcome is unacceptable, you need to revise your functional plans, revise your programs, revise your strategies (including reconsidering your business definition and/or your business model), and/or revise your survival goals. Then, once again, look at the expected outcomes. In other words, arriving at an actionable survival plan is an iterative process: plan, test, revise and test again— until you are satisfied with the results.

And once you have done this, you should have a survival plan that defines what will move you along your chosen path and identifies who will do what along the way. You also will be assured that the path you have chosen provides you with a reasonable chance of reaching your destination.

Documenting the Plan

Now, that you have verified that your plan does lead to your key survival goals, that you do have (or have access to) all of the resources needed for the plan (cash, capital, skills), and that there are no other business constraints that will prevent your plan from being successful; you are ready to document your overall Survival Action Plan.

Of course you could skip creating such a document and approach business survival one program and one action at a time. However, assuming that you have developed a number of actions that together comprise your business survival plan, we strongly recommend that you document these actions in a way that presents a compelling story.

Why is this important? This document, if written and communicated properly, can be key to selling the important survival actions to your organization. In other words, this document can be a critical tool for motivating and effectively re–directing the energy of your team in the desired direction. And this document, coupled with a process/methodology for monitoring results, provides the framework for coordinating efforts and for making and implementing mid–course corrections to keep you on the track to business survival, stabilization, and ultimately turnaround.

To say it another way, a Survival Action Plan Document has three primary goals: 1) to communicate the magnitude of the problems and to describe and justify the chosen survival actions, 2) to create a sense of urgency and gain the support of your organization for implementation of these actions, and 3) to provide a framework for coordinating efforts, monitoring survival progress and making mid–course corrections.

So what are the components of an effective Survival Action Plan Document? This document has some similarities to a comprehensive Business Plan, but there is a key difference. The intended audience of a Survival Action Plan is primarily internal—your own organization. As such it doesn't need to contain detailed company, business, and/or market background information. In addition, to accomplish the primary goals, a Survival Action Plan Document should:

- Focus on business survival (results) in the relatively short–to–medium–term

- Clearly describe the specific business crisis and define what survival means

- Highlight the basic business changes needed for survival and justify these changes

- Define specific priorities and actions, including responsibility assignments

Figure 5–3 below shows our suggested outline for such a document.

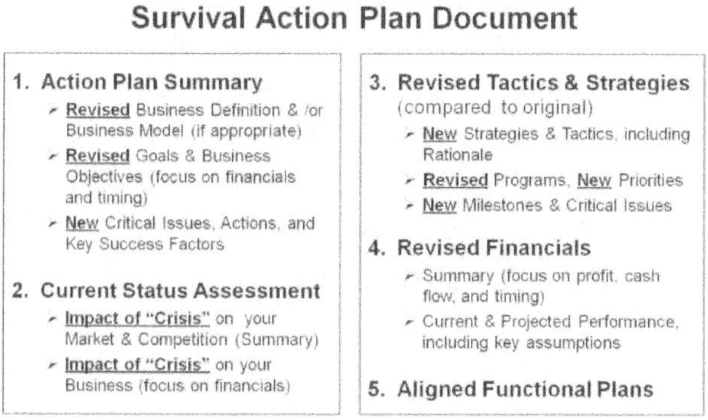

Survival Action Plan Document

1. Action Plan Summary
- ➤ **Revised** Business Definition & /or Business Model (if appropriate)
- ➤ **Revised** Goals & Business Objectives (focus on financials and timing)
- ➤ **New** Critical Issues, Actions, and Key Success Factors

2. Current Status Assessment
- ➤ **Impact of "Crisis"** on your Market & Competition (Summary)
- ➤ **Impact of "Crisis"** on your Business (focus on financials)

3. Revised Tactics & Strategies
(compared to original)
- ➤ **New** Strategies & Tactics, including Rationale
- ➤ **Revised** Programs, **New** Priorities
- ➤ **New** Milestones & Critical Issues

4. Revised Financials
- ➤ Summary (focus on profit, cash flow, and timing)
- ➤ Current & Projected Performance, including key assumptions

5. Aligned Functional Plans

FIGURE 5–3: SURVIVAL ACTION PLAN DOCUMENT

Remember, this is a document intended only for internal use, so includes minimal background information. It summarizes the key points that will allow you to clearly and convincingly communicate the important elements of your planned survival actions, along with the supporting financial information, to your organization. Following, each section is described in more detail.

ACTION PLAN SUMMARY. This section establishes the business boundaries (existing or revised) and defines the survival Goals and Objectives (usually financial. It should describe clearly what is being changed from your existing plan and should convey the importance of timing. The key cost/spending containment actions, including any downsizing, and any business rationalization and/or redirection actions should be specifically described. The critical issues and key success factors should convey the seriousness of your business situation.

CURRENT STATUS ASSESSMENT. This provides a realistic and current business Baseline for your organization. It should clearly illustrate how the economy has impacted your market, your competition, and your business, with emphasis on the financial situation. Bottom line, it provides the justification and sense of urgency for the planned changes.

REVISED TACTICS AND STRATEGIES. This section compares the survival tactics/strategies to the original ones, and provides justification for the new ones. Of particular importance are the revised program priorities and milestones, including revised functional plans for addressing the new priorities.

REVISED FINANCIALS. This section is fairly self explanatory. However, an explanation of why there needs to be a focus on profit and cash flow can be useful for gaining support for the plan.

ALIGNED FUNCTIONAL PLANS. This section of the Survival Action Plan summarizes the revised plans that each Function has developed to combat the business crisis. As stated in the previous section, each functional plan must be consistent with the overall survival plan and with the plans of the other functions. Note: To keep functional plans aligned requires continuing communication and feedback among the Functions. It needs to be emphasized that this is a coordinated, business *team* effort.

Now, assuming that the Survival Action Plan has been clearly documented, the challenge for leadership is effectively implementing that plan. In other words the challenge is making change happen.

MAKING CHANGE HAPPEN

An effective leader is important for success in almost any team sport, but is essential when playing the ultimate team game of business survival.

Implementing a Survival Action Plan means making change happen. And this is a complicated and sometimes controversial business topic which is not limited to times of crisis. It has been covered in depth by many books and papers under the topic "the management of change." Because of its complexity, we feel that doing justice to this aspect of leadership is beyond the scope of our book. However, in this section we do provide perspectives on several areas that we consider key success factors for implementing change.

MANAGEMENT TEAM. You, the business leader, have many demanding responsibilities in times of crisis. Therefore it is essential that you have a competent and dedicated management team to assist you in the planning and implementation of the necessary survival actions. And, we strongly recommend that you assign one member of your management team to provide you with specific assistance.

RESOURCES/SUPPORT. Without adequate resources and internal support for the necessary actions (often including downsizing and/or outsourcing), your business survival plan and your business are doomed to failure. We assume that you already have the needed resources or have access to them (part of developing a realistic survival action plan). However it is likely that obtaining the needed support from your organization will depend on your ability to "sell" your survival plan to your management team and your employees. This often comes down to creating a compelling document and presenting it in a convincing way—to your own organization. And this, of course, is your Survival Action Plan document.

LEADERSHIP. An effective leader is essential for the success of almost any team endeavor, and implementation of a Survival Action Plan is certainly a "team sport". Although there are many attributes that contribute to effective leadership, in the case of action plan implementation, providing consistent direction and making sure messages are unambiguous are keys. In addition, creating a sense of urgency but not one of desperation is important.

COMMUNICATION. This starts with clear *downward* communication of the key elements of the Survival Action Plan to the entire organization. But that is only the beginning. There needs to be: rapid and complete *sideways* communication across the organization to keep actions coordinated, clear *upward* communication related to progress/obstacles, and appropriate sharing of information both inside and outside of the organization with people having a need–to– know. It's impossible to overstress the importance of continuing leadership communication in difficult times.

RESPONSIBILITIES. All employees must have clearly assigned responsibilities and expectations. And it is equally important to clarify to the *entire* organization who has responsibility for making what decisions and who has responsibility for implementing those decisions. In addition, it is essential that the necessary resources are dedicated to the priority programs—always a leadership challenge to make sure that this happens.

MOTIVATION. Presenting a compelling case for the Survival Action Plan is a part of motivating employees and gaining their support. It's not necessary that everyone agrees with all of the actions, but it is important that they understand the actions and the rationale for them. And conveying enthusiasm and hope in difficult situations is always important.

ORGANIZATION. Often leaders focus on re–organization and restructuring as the only solution to plan execution. Having the right organization is important, particularly if downsizing or outsourcing is one of the actions, but the other factors summarized above are just as important—and sometimes they are even more important.

For a more in–depth look at issues and suggested approaches for making change happen, we suggest the articles and books in Reference (68). They provide different perspectives on making change happen, including examples.

However, making change happen isn't the end. The ability to rapidly adapt survival plans and actions to a chaotic business and economic landscape is essential. And that is what *"Dynamic Business Leadership"* is all about—our concluding topic.

Chapter 6

Dynamic Business Leadership

Although we have explored various survival actions, tactics, and strategies in this book; business survival in chaotic times is really all about leadership. But chaotic times require a specific kind of leadership—what we are calling *"Dynamic Business Leadership."* We summarized some of the characteristics of this type of leader in the Introduction, but in this chapter we highlight in more detail the key elements and challenges involved. Then we conclude this chapter and our book by focusing on business survival through continuing and adaptive leadership actions. The methodology we suggest for accomplishing this is the *"Living Action Plan."*

KEY LEADERSHIP ELEMENTS

> *In a crisis, nothing guarantees business survival, but without a dynamic leader the business ship is doomed.*

What is *"Dynamic Business Leadership"*? It is a combination of leadership actions for riding the waves of economic chaos. To paraphrase our words from the Introduction:

> *"Think about a business leader as the captain of a ship. When navigating in calm seas, the captain can reach the desired destination by relying on experience and directions from the stars. However, to survive in stormy and foggy weather, the captain must rapidly make and implement critical, life–saving decisions. The captain also needs to use modern navigation tools for frequent course corrections to have a reasonable chance of guiding his/her ship through treacherous and unfamiliar waters."*

In today's disruptive economic environment, leading a business to "safe shores" is much the same. In a crisis, nothing guarantees business survival and stability, but chances for success can be optimized through a multi–component approach that characterizes dynamic business leadership. This approach consists of the five types of leadership actions highlighted below in *Figure 6–1* and described in the remainder of this section.

Leadership for Business Survival

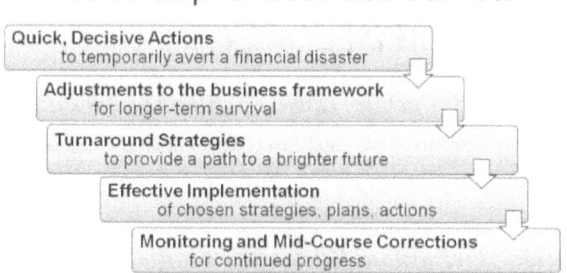

FIGURE 6–1: DYNAMIC LEADERSHIP FOR BUSINESS SURVIVAL

First there are the *quick, decisive actions* intended to temporarily avert a financial disaster and save the basic business from the imminent, life–threatening economic forces (stop the business ship from sinking). Based on an assessment of the financial situation and market dynamics, these are of two types: internally focused actions that usually address cost/spending containment and minimizing investments (damage control from Chapter 1) and externally focused actions include pricing optimization, sales promotions, and advertising spending (the rapid defensive moves from Chapter 2). However, whether the focus is internal or external, the timeframe is immediate and the goal is business stabilization.

The next set of actions makes *adjustments* to the business framework for survival (keeps the business ship afloat). These actions are those that we called short–term survival tactics in Chapter 3. The first steps include defining survival for the business, and then making changes to the business goals and the business model to be consistent with those decisions.

Subsequent actions may include layoffs, product and/or business rationalization, sourcing or other business model changes, and program prioritization. The timeframe for some of these types of actions may be relatively short–term, but others require a longer time. So from our perspective, the timeframe for most actions focused on business survival usually ranges from a few months to as much as a year or longer.

Development of *turnaround strategies* to provide a path to a viable and brighter future (optimizes chances for survival and growth once "safe" shores have been reached) is the third type of leadership action. These are strategies for sustaining and growing the business in the changed world on the other side of the economic storm. They include somewhat longer–term actions such as business expansion to new customers, new products, changing the business definition to accommodate new businesses, and alliances and acquisitions (Chapter 4).

Effective implementation of chosen actions, strategies, plans (puts it all together to make headway toward the distant shore) has no timeframe, but generally speaking, the sooner the better. Making the best decisions, taking immediate action, developing a detailed and coordinated Survival Action Plan, and seeing that the necessary actions to implement that plan are taken. These are key challenges at any time for a business "captain" (Chapter 5), but are particularly important in times of crisis.

However there is one additional important set of leadership actions: those actions focused on *monitoring and mid–Course Corrections* for continued progress (keeping the business moving in the right direction, towards safety). Continuous monitoring of your business environment and of the results from implementing your Survival Action Plan (both short–term and longer–term actions) and use of that information to make frequent business course corrections are necessary components of business survival in a dynamic world. The methodology we suggest for accomplishing this is the subject of our next and last section—the "*Living*" Action Plan.

THE "LIVING" ACTION PLAN

Business survival in a dynamic world
requires a dynamic action plan.

A *"Living"* Action Plan is one that evolves and can be adapted quickly to changing business situations. It not only is an action–oriented document, but also is a process whereby plan revisions can be made and effectively implemented as circumstances dictate. What the plan changes are and how rapidly they need to be implemented determine how drastic the accompanying actions must be.

Why do you need a *living* plan? To quote from Chapter 1 in our book "DYNAMIC BUSINESS PLANNING BASICS" (2):

"New competitors are being born, customer requirements evolve, technology advances, the economy changes, disasters happen, and so on. To be relevant in this dynamic business environment, your plan also needs to be dynamic. Aiming toward a Goal with a "fixed" plan is like trying to drive a car without steering. At best you are likely to end up at an unexpected destination. At the worst, you will drive off a cliff."

To say it another way: Creating, documenting, and implementing a Survival Action Plan encompassing both the short–term and the longer–term is not a one–time event in today's chaotic environment. Fighting for business survival in the midst of continuing disruptive economic changes is a challenge, and that challenge is likely to require timely revisions to any survival plan.

So how can crises caused by plan obsolescence be avoided? We suggest adopting a cyclic process that results in a *"living"* plan. Whether this is a basic business plan or a Survival Action Plan, this process consists of four stages: 1) *Execute* the plan, 2) *Monitor* the results, 3) *Analyze* the problems, and 4) *Revise* the plan. And then, *REPEAT THE PROCESS.*

Figure 6–2 below illustrates this cycle that turns your Survival Action Plan into a "living" one. The remainder of this section describes each step in some detail.

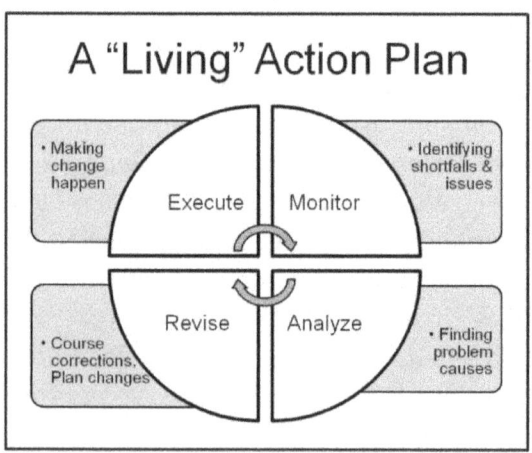

FIGURE 6–2: THE "LIVING" ACTION PLAN CYCLE

The first (and the last) step in this cycle, EXECUTE (or Implement), is all about making change happen. This was addressed in the previous chapter, so won't be repeated here.

The second step is <u>MONITOR</u>. Accurate monitoring of your business performance and of changes in your market is essential in order to identify the shortfalls and issues related to your survival goals and actions. This involves creating and using a periodic review process to track actual results and then compare them to "expected results" from your Action Plan. As a starting point, we suggest these areas as ones that commonly need review:

- Market Dynamics, including demand changes and competitive actions and reactions
- Financials
- Program Milestones/Schedules
- Expected results from survival actions and tactics

However, it is up to you to pick your specific focus areas and then create the review process. We strongly suggest that you consider frequent reviews (at least once a month) since the business landscape can change rapidly in times of economic chaos. In addition, when structuring a review process it is important to: identify the reviewers, establish the review format, and specify the data to be presented and compared to the targets for each particular area being reviewed.

We also suggest that you create a simple, graphic way of showing progress/results versus expectations. For example, a color–coded template based on an Excel spreadsheet can serve as this kind of an updatable "dashboard" or "scorecard". If you don't want to create your own, there are many variations available on the internet (just search terms such as "dashboard template" or "business scorecard").

The outcomes from this review process should include the identification of shortfalls, specific problems, and critical issues. Examples of typical issues/problems that arise during action plan execution are things such as:

- Programs falling behind schedule
- Unanticipated shortage of cash or other resources
- Low sales volumes and/or high manufacturing costs
- Inability to find suitable partners/alliances
- Poor financial results compared to expectations

In the ANALYZE step of the cycle the "root" causes of the problems and issues identified in the Monitoring step are determined. Another more technical name for this process is "deviation analysis". With this information in hand, you can move to the fourth step in the cycle—making revisions.

REVISE. Revisions generally fall into two categories—mid–course corrections and Action Plan changes. Typically mid–course corrections address internal and/or organizational issues such as poor project management skills, lack of effective prioritization, lack of functional alignment (see Chapter 5), and productivity. These kinds of corrections do not necessarily require significant action plan revisions.

However, unanticipated occurrences often do require updating/revising the Action Plan or sometimes even abandoning the current plan and developing a new one. Examples of these types of issues include mis–calculation of costs and/or capabilities, unexpected competition or other market changes, increased pressure from external forces outside your control (e.g., recession turning into a depression, earthquakes, revolutions, etc.), or other insurmountable obstacles such as technology inadequacy or major program timing issues.

Based on your monitoring results, you should be able to determine whether you need mid–course corrections and/or basic plan revisions. Once you have made the appropriate Action Plan revisions, you have completed the final step in the cycle. And you are ready to continue on again to the first step of the cycle: Executing your "Living" Action Plan.

CONCLUSION

> *"...turbulence, and especially heightened turbulence, with its consequent chaos, risk, and uncertainty, is now the normal condition of industries, markets, and companies."*
> *(69a)*

Recession, revolution, earthquake, tsunami, and more. Is it over yet? Can business leaders relax and return to "what always has worked?" Probably not.

In this turbulent new world of the 21st century, whatever the cause and the magnitude of the business crisis, survival will require a new kind of leadership— what we have called *Dynamic Business Leadership*. Today and tomorrow and the day after that, we believe that this kind of leadership will be the key to business success in the treacherous sea of economic chaos.

For additional reading about leadership in our disruptive environment, we suggest the books in References (13) and (69). In addition, the two internet articles in Reference (70) provide good summary information.

Management Guidance for
Disruptive Times

REFERENCES

Introduction

1. For an in–depth look at the recessions and business:
   a. *The Return of Recession Economics and the Crisis of 2008*, P. Krugman, W.W. Norton and Company, 2009
   b. *Recessions and Depressions: Understanding Business Cycles*, T. Knoop, Praeger, 2nd Edition, 2009

Chapter 1

2. For information on business assessments and establishing a business baseline see *Dynamic Business Planning Basics: An Adaptable Planning Process for Disruptive Times*, C. Fatuzzo and E. Fatuzzo, CreateSpace 2010
3. Summary descriptions of cash flow:
   a. www.en.wikipedia.org/wiki/Cash_flow
   b. www.investopedia.com/articles/04/033104.asp?viewed=1
4. A more in–depth look at cash flow and managing cash:
   a. *Essentials of Cash Flow*, H. Schaeffer Jr., Wiley 1st edition, 2002
   b. *Managing Cash Flow: An Operational Focus*, R. Reider and P. Heyler, Wiley, 2002
   c. *Small Business Cash Flow: Strategies for Making Your Business a Financial Success*, D. O"Berry, Wiley, 2006
5. For overviews of the current business environment and the important of cash:
   a. "Desperately seeking a cash cure", *The Economist*, November 20, 2008, available at: www.economist.com/finance/displaystory.cfm?story_id =12636353

b. "Don't Let the Downturn Get You Down", *Business Week*, February 20, 2008, available at: www.businessweek.com/magazine/content/08_62/s0802 042617557.htm

6. *Cut Costs + Grow Stronger: A Strategic Approach to What to Cut and What to Keep*, S. Banerjii, P. Leinwand, and C. Mainardi, Harvard Business Press, 2010 (Kindle edition, Section 1)

7. "Cutting Costs Without Drawing Blood," T. Copeland, *Harvard Business Review*, September–October 2000

8. For additional perspectives on cost cutting and investments in recessionary times see Reference (7) and:
   a. "The Risk of Not Investing in a Recession," Pankaj Ghemawat, *Sloan Management Review*, Winter 1993
   b. "A Better Way to Cut Costs," Rita McGrath, *Harvard Business Review Blog*, March 9, 2009, available at: http://blogs.hbr.org/hbr/mcgrath/2009/03/a–better–way–to–cut–costs.html

9. For more in depth information on cost cutting/containment see Reference (6) and:
   a. *Driving Down Cost*, A. Wileman, Nicholas Brealey Publishing, London, 2008
   b. *Cost Containment: The Ultimate Advantage*, P. Richardson, The Free Press, New York, 1988
   c. *Cost Reduction and Control Best Practices: The Best Ways for a Financial Manager to Save Money (Wiley Best Practices)*, Institute of Management and Administration, Wiley 2nd Edition, 2005
   d. *A Manager's Guide to Creative Cost Cutting*, D. Young, McGraw–Hill, 2002

Chapter 2

10. "How to Think about Pricing Strategies in a Downturn," N. Wreden, *Harvard Management Update*, March 2002

11. "Will the Hard–Core Starbucks Customer Pay More? The Chain Plans to Find Out," C. Miller, *The New York Times*, August 21, 2009, available at: www.nytimes.com/2009/08/21/business/21sbux.html?_r=2

12. Basic internet information about price elasticity and demand:
    a. http://en.wikipedia.org/wiki/Price_elasticity_of_demand
    b. www.netmba.com/econ/micro/demand/elasticity/price/
    c. http://economics.about.com/cs/micfrohelp/a/priceelasticity.htm

13. *Recession Storming: Thriving in Downturns through Superior Marketing, Pricing, and Product Strategies*, R. Hart, distributed through Amazon.com, 2008

14. For basic information on demand cross elasticity see: http://en.wikipedia.org/wiki/Cross_elasticity_of_demand

15. A summary of key factors to consider: "Pricing Strategies for the Downturn" by P. Nunes, *Harvard Business Review Blog*, March 2009, available at: http://blogs.hbr.org/cs/2009/03/pricing_strategies_for_the_dow.html

16. A sampling of internet based general information:
    a. "Choosing the Wrong Pricing Strategy Can be a Costly Mistake": http://knowledge.wharton.upenn.edu/article.cfm?articleid=792
    b. The website: http://www.netmba.com/marketing/pricing/

17. For additional information and different perspectives on pricing, see:
    a. "How to Fight a Price War," A. Rao, M. Bergen, and S. Davis, *Harvard Business Review*, March–April 2000
    b. *The Upside of the Downturn: Ten Management Strategies to Prevail in the Recession and Thrive in the Aftermath*, G. Colvin, "Chapter 9: Price with Courage," Portfolio (Penguin Books) 2009
    c. *Pricing with Confidence: 10 Ways to Stop Leaving Money on the Table*, R. Holden and M. Burton, John Wiley and Sons, Hoboken, NJ 2008 (provides some simple "rules" for pricing in challenging economic times)
    d. *Harvard Business Review on Pricing*, Harvard Business School Publishing, Boston, MA, 2008 (a collection of relevant articles)

e. *Competitive Advantage: Creating and Sustaining Superior Performance*, M. Porter, The Free Press, 1985 (considered a landmark text on competition)

18. An example of the impact of a pricing related sales promotion:

   a. "Online Sales Rose 15% this Holiday, Beating In–Store Growth this Report Says," T. Williams, *The New York Times*, December 23, 2010, available at: www.nytimes.com/2010/12/24/business/24retail.html

   b. "Gift Shopper Flocked to the Web," *The Wall Street Journal*, December 24, 2010, available at: http://online.wsj.com/article/SB100014240527487035486045760380518168009900.html?KEYWORDS=december+web+sales

19. "Wal–Mart Says 'Try This On': Free Shipping," S. Clifford and C. Miller, *The New York Times*, November 11, 2010, available at: www.nytimes.com/2010/11/11/business/11shipping.html?scp=1&sq=walmart%20free%20shipping&st=cse

20. Examples of promotions and pricing strategies intertwined:

   a. "Wal–Mart Wins Big During Downturn," C. Palmeri, *Business Week*, October 30, 2008, available at: www.businessweek.com/magazine/content/08_45/b4107034210776.htm

   b. "Pricing: How Low can you Really Go?," R. McCarthy, *inc.com*, March 2009, available at: www.inc.com/magazine/20090301/pricing–how–low–can–you–really–go.html

   c. "In Recession Specials, Small Firms Revise Pricing," D. Mattioli, *The Wall Street Journal*, 2009, available at: http://online.wsj.com/article/SB124449716827695585.html

21. For a summary of various marketing studies relating to advertising spending see: "Spending MarCom Dollars During a Recession Reaps Revenue Benefits Now . . . and Later!," *allerton.com newsletter*, June 2009, available at: www.allerton.com/newsletter/SpendingMarComDollarsDuringaRecession.pdf

22. Detailed marketing studies on advertising in recessionary times:
    a. "Should Firms Spend More On R&D And Advertising During Recessions?," R. Srinivasan, G. Lilien, and S. Sridhar, *Journal of Marketing*, October 29, 2010, available at: www.marketingpower.com/AboutAMA/Documents/JM_Forthcoming/should_firms_spend_more_on.pdf
    b. "Should Firms Increase Advertising Expenditures during Recessions?," K. Frankenberger and R. Graham, *Marketing Science Institute*, 2003, available at: www.msi.org/publications/publication.cfm?pub=662

23. For a good perspective on why to spend on advertising see: "When the Going Gets Tough, the Tough Don't Skimp on Their Ad Budgets", *Knowledge@Wharton*, November, 26, 2008, available at: http://knowledge.wharton.upenn.edu/article.cfm?articleid=2101#

24. Examples and suggestions relating to advertising in difficult economic times:
    a. "Is Recession the Time to Boost Ad Spending?," J. Scanlon, *Bloomberg Businessweek*, May 1, 2009, available at: www.businessweek.com/innovate/content/may2009/id2009051_889327.htm
    b. "Top 100 Outlays Plunge 10% but Defying Spend Trend Can Pay Off," B. Johnson, *Advertising Age*, June 21, 2010, available at: http://adage.com/article?article_id=144555
    c. "Advertising During a Recession", ARSgroup, 2008, available at: www.iirusa.com/upload/wysiwyg/2008–M–Div/M2028/pdfs/Advertising–During–a–Recession.pdf

25. More general marketing advice for difficult economic times:
    a. "How to Market in a Recession," J. Quelch, *Harvard Business Review Blog*, September 24, 2008 available at: http://blogs.hbr.org/quelch/2008/09/how_to_market_in_a_recession.html

b. "Marketing in a Recession: 10 Things to Remember," L. Evans, HDE Agency, June 2009, available at: www.hdeagency.com/blog/?p=13

Chapter 3

26. Major layoffs between December 2007 and July 2010: "The Layoff Kings: The 25 Companies Responsible for 700,000 Lost Jobs," D. Mcintyre, *Daily Finance*, August 18, 2010, available at: www.dailyfinance.com/story/the–layoff–kings–the–25–companies–responsible–for–700–000–lost/19588515/

27. Different perspectives on downsizing:
    a. "The Hidden Leverage of Human Capital," J. Oxman, *Sloan Management Review*, Summer 2002
    b. "Cutting Costs to Increase Profits," B. Steverman, *Business Week*, November 25, 2008, available at: www.businessweek.com/print/investor/content/nov2008/pi20081124_520205.htm
    c. "As Layoffs Spread, Innovative Alternatives May Soften the Blow," available at: http://knowledge.wharton.upenn.edu/article.cfm?articleid=2106

28. For useful insights on layoffs: *Responsible Restructuring: Creative and Profitable Alternatives to Layoffs*, W. Cascio, Berrett–Koehler Publishers, San Francisco, CA, 2002

29. "The Future of Outsourcing," *Bloomberg Business Week*, January 30, 2006, available at: www.businessweek.com/magazine/content/06_05/b3969401.htm

30. For additional information about organizational productivity, see:
    a. *Business Restructuring: An Action Template for Reducing Cost and Growing Profit*, C. Zilka, Wiley, 2009
    b. *Corporate Restructuring: From Cause Analysis to Execution*, D. Vance, Springer, 2009

31. Internet references describing business models and providing examples:
    a. Wikipedia: http://en.wikipedia.org/wiki/Business_model
    b. QuickMBA: www.quickmba.com/entre/business–model/

32. Provides an in–depth look at business models and their importance: "Why Business Models Matter," J. Magretta, *Harvard Business Review*, May 1, 2002

33. "Current" examples of business model revisions and their benefits:

   a. Business model revision combined with other cost cutting actions: "Cost Cutting Helps Dell Profit Exceed Forecasts," A. Vance, *The New York Times*, November 21, 2008, available at: www.nytimes.com/2008/11/21/technology/companies/21 dell.html?th&emc=th

   b. The evolution of a company that has successfully used business model revision to improve its performance – over and over: "Amazon's Smart Innovation Strategy," M. Johnson, *Bloomberg Businessweek*, April 12, 2010, available at: www.businessweek.com/innovate/content/apr2010/id20 100412_520351.htm

   c. Apple – a shift in focus from product to "platform" : www.nytimes.com/2011/01/30/business/30unbox.html?_ r=1&nl=todaysheadlines&emc=tha26

34. Useful articles and book chapters relating to revising business models:

   a. "Spotlight on Business Model Innovation", *Harvard Business Review*, January–February 2011

   b. "What are Business Models and How are They Built?," C. Christensen and M. Johnson, *Harvard Business Press Module note*, August 10, 2009

   c. "Reinventing Your Business Model," C. Christensen, M. Johnson, and H. Kagermann, *Harvard Business Review*, December 1, 2008

   d. "Why Companies Should Have Open Business Models," H. Chesbrough, *Harvard Business Review*, January 1, 2007

   e. *Getting the Scope of the Business Right*, C. Christensen and M. Raynor, Book Chapter, Harvard Business School Press, September 3, 2003

35. Current books and basic references on business models

    a. *Open Business Models: How to Thrive in the New Innovation Landscape*, H. Chesbrough, Harvard Business Press, 2006

    b. *The Ultimate Competitive Advantage: Secrets of Continually Developing a More Profitable Business Model*, D. Mitchell, C. Coles, B. Golisano, and R. Knutson; Berrett–Koehler Publishers; San Francisco CA 2003

    c. *Business Models: A Strategic Management Approach*, A. Afuah, McGraw–Hill/Irwin, New York, NY 2003

    d. *Business Model Generation: A Handbook for Visionaries, Game Changers, and Challengers*, A. Osterwalder, Wiley & Sons, 2010

    e. *Seizing the White Space: Business Model Innovation for Growth and Renewal*, A. Lafley and M. Johnson, Harvard Business Press, 2010

    f. *Business Models made Easy*, D. Debelak, Entrepreneur Press, 2006

    g. *Harvard Business Review on Business Model Innovation (Harvard Business Review Paperback Series)*, Harvard Business Press, 2010

36. For an accepted way to evaluate R&D programs see: "Is It Real? Can We Win? Is It Worth Doing? (Managing Risk and Reward in an Innovation Portfolio)," G. Day, *Harvard Business Review*, December 2007

37. For detailed information related to R&D program evaluation and prioritization, see: *Portfolio Management for New Products*, R. Cooper, S. Edgett, and E. Kleinschmidt, Second Edition, Basic Books, New York, NY, 2001

38. For information on using a "scorecard" approach and other techniques for program evaluation, see: *Project Leadership*, R. Cooper, Chapter 5, Second Edition, Basic Books, New York, NY 2005

39. For insight into innovation and new products during a recession see:

    a. "Innovation in a Recession," *Bloomberg Businessweek,* Special Report, July 22, 2009, available at: www.businessweek.com/innovate/di_special/20090722i nnovation_in_a_recession.htm

b. "It's No Time to Forget About Innovation," J. Rae–Dupree, *The New York Times*, November 2, 2008, available at: www.nytimes.com/2008/11/02/business/02unbox.html?scp=1&sq=Rae–&st=nyt

Chapter 4

40. "The Right Game: Use Game Theory to Shape Strategy," A. Brandenburger and B. Nalebuff, *Harvard Business Review*, July–August 1995
41. Porter's 5 Forces Model:
    a. quickmba: www.quickmba.com/strategy/porter.shtml
    b. *Competitive Advantage: Creating and sustaining Superior Performance,* M. Porter, The Free Press 1985
42. *Competitive Strategy: Techniques for analyzing Industries and Competitors*, M. Porter, Chapter 2, The Free Press 1980
43. For details on the business game and game–changing actions see: *Co–opetition: A revolutionary mindset that combines competition and cooperation. The Game Theory Strategy that's changing the game of business*, A. Brandenburger and B. Nalebuff, Doubleday, New York, NY, 1996" (A landmark book which uses the principles of Game Theory for developing business strategies. It teaches the "game" of business and how to change that game)
44. "7–Eleven Sees an Opportunity to Open Doors," J. LeVere, *The New York Times*, July 14, 2009, available at: www.nytimes.com/2009/07/15/realestate/commercial/15seven.html?_r=1
45. Starbucks and new customers:
    a. "Starbucks Targets Regular Joes," K. Helliker, *The Wall Street Journal*, May 12, 2010, available at: http://online.wsj.com/article/SB100014240527487035658045752385842046653378.html?mod=e2tw
    b. "For Starbucks, a New Retail Mix," J. Jargon, *The Wall Street Journal*, August 18, 2010, available at: http://online.wsj.com/article/SB100014240527487045577045754377301489951528.html?KEYWORDS=starbucks
46. New Product Priorities and Acceleration:

a. *Winning at New Products: Accelerating the Process from Idea to Launch*, R. Cooper, Third Edition, Perseus Publishing, Cambridge, MA, 2001

b. *Developing Products in Half the Time*, P. Smith and D. Reinertsen, Van Nostrand Reinhold, New York, NY, 1991

47. "Ten Retailers Turning Department Stores Into Mini–Malls," M. Cardona, *DailyFinance*, available at www.dailyfinance.com/story/company–news/in–store–shops–in–department–stores/19694054/?icid=main%7Chtmlws–sb–n%7Cdl3%7Csec1_lnk3%7C183213

48. For descriptions of "Business Definition" see:

a. "Building Your Brand Part 1: Defining Your Business Purpose," D. Wilson, available at: www.wilsonweb.com/tools/danwilson–defining–purpose.htm

b. www.12manage.com/methods_abell_three_dimensional_business_definition.html

49. For Internet Articles relating to the importance of your Business Definition see:

a. "Competitive and performance implications of business definitions," Noel Houthoofd, *AllBusiness*, June 22, 2006, available at: www.allbusiness.com/management/3956992–1.html

b. "Expanding Your Business: It's About Your Values," C. Hemingway and A. Rubinfeld, *Wharton School Publishing*, May 20, 2005, available at: www.whartonsp.com/articles/article.aspx?p=373336

c. "defining the business mission," allen u, October 2010, available at: http://e–articles.info/e/a/title/Defining–the–Business–Mission/

50. For basic references on Business Definition and performance see:

a. "Business Definition and Performance," G. Frazier and R. Howell, *Journal of Marketing*, Vol. 47 (Spring 1983), 59–67

b. "Strategic Innovation," C. Markides, *MIT Sloan Management Review*, April 15, 1997

    c. *Process to Profits: Strategic Planning for a Growing Business*, W. Lasher, Thompson Corporation (Mason, Ohio) 2005

51. Business expansion through acquisition—an example: "Dells 'Reshaping' of PC Maker Means Chasing Services," C. Guglielmo, *Bloomberg Business Week*, October 16, 2009, available at: www.bloomberg.com/apps/news?pid=20601109&sid=aK7wd aUAkkBo

52. Business expansion through innovation—an example: "Can Amazon be the Wal–Mart of the Web?," B. Stone, *The New York Times*, September 19, 2009, available at: www.nytimes.com/2009/09/20/business/20amazon.html?th& emc=th

53. Program/Business evaluation methodologies: "How 3M Evaluates its R&D Programs," L. Krogh, J. Prager, D. Sorensen, and J. Tomlinson, *Research Technology Management*, November–December 1988

54. Growth through new business: "The Untold Story: How the iPhone Blew Up the Wireless Industry," F. Vogelstein, *Wired Magazine*, January 2008, available at: www.wired.com/gadgets/wireless/magazine/16– 02/ff_iphone?currentPage=1

55. RCA's new business acquisitions: http://en.wikipedia.org/wiki/Radio_Corporation_of_America

56. The challenges of alliances and acquisitions: *Strategic Alliances: Three Ways to Make Them Work (Memo to the CEO)*, S. Steinhilber, Harvard Business School Press, Boston, MA, 2008.

57. Additional insights and perspectives on turnaround strategies:
    a. "Strategies to prevent economic recessions from causing business failure," J. Pearce II and S. Michael, *Business Horizons* (Indiana University Kelley School of Business), 2006, volume 49
    b. "Moving Upward in a Downturn," D. Rigby, *Harvard Business Review*, June 2001
    c. "In Hard Times, Is Best Buy's Best Good Enough?," L. Fromm, *The New York Times*, December, 7, 2008,

available at:
www.nytimes.com/2008/12/07/business/07best.html?_r
=1&scp=4&sq=Laura%20Fromm&st=cse

d. "Bring on the Recession: It's the Best Time to Strengthen Your Strategic Position," R. Atkins and A. Slywotzky: www.lippincottmercer.com/publications/b_atkins.shtml

Chapter 5

58. *The Future of Management*, G. Hamel, Harvard Business School Press, 2007

59. For books and articles on the value of science–based decision–making and leadership, see:

a. "Don't Trust Your Gut," E. Bonabeau, *Harvard Business Review*, May 2003

b. *Competing on Analytics: The New Science of Winning*, T. Davenport and J. Harris, Harvard Business School Press, Boston, MA, 2007

c. *Adaptive Business Intelligence*, Z. Michalewicz, M. Schmidt, M. Michalewicz, and C. Chirac, Springer, New York, NY, 2007

d. *Harvard Business Review on Managing Uncertainty*, Harvard Business School Press, Boston, MA, 1999 (collection of articles)

e. *Thinking Strategically: The Competitive Edge in Business, Politics, and Everyday Life*, A. Dixit and B. Nalebuff, W.W. Norton and Company, New York, NY, 1993

f. *Wargaming for Leaders: Strategic Decision Making from the Battlefield to the Boardroom*, M. Herman, M. Frost, and R. Kurz, McGraw–Hill, New York, NY, 2009

g. *Super Crunchers: Why Thinking–by–numbers is the New Way to be Smart*, I. Ayres, Bantam Books, New York, NY, 2007

h. *Science Lessons: What the Business of Biotech Taught me about Management*, G. Binder, Harvard Business Press, Boston, MA, 2008

60. For a somewhat technical description of the basics of Game Theory for the non–expert with easy–to–understand examples of different business "games" see: *Game Theory at*

Work: How to use Game Theory to outthink and outmaneuver your competition, J. Miller, McGraw–Hill, New York, NY, 2003

61. Additional information about Game Theory for business see Reference and:

   a. *Games, Strategies, & Managers: How Managers can use Game Theory to make better business decisions*, J. McMillan, Oxford University Press, New York, NY, 1992 (A very readable, nontechnical book that applies the general principles and logic of Game Theory to basic business decision–making. A good introduction to the concept of Game Theory for business.)

   b. *Games Businesses Play: Cases and Models*, P. Ghemawat, the MIT Press, Cambridge, MA, 1998 (Uses detailed case studies and examples of actual business interactions to explore the uses and limits of quantitative Game Theory as a strategic decision–making tool.   More analytical and less descriptive than some of the other references.)

   c. *Game Theory, a Critical Introduction*, S. Hargreaves–Heap and Y. Varoufakis, Routledge, New York, NY, 1995 (More of an academic introduction, but relatively non–technical. Good descriptions of the elements of Game Theory and the different types of games.)

62. For consulting firms specializing in Game Theory see: www.gametheory.net/links/consulting.html

63. For introductions to and explanations of ABMS see:

   a. *The Complexity of Cooperation: Agent–Based Models of Competition and Collaboration*, R. Axelrod, Princeton University Press, Princeton, NJ, 1997 (Provides a historical perspective of ABMS)

   b. *Agent–Based Models*, N. Gilbert, Sage Publications, Thousand Oaks, CA, 2008 (Contains examples of different applications of ABMS in the social sciences)

   c. *Managing Business Complexity: Discovering Strategic Solutions with Agent–Based Modeling and Simulation*, M. North and C. Macal, Oxford University Press, New York, NY, 2007 (A more "complete" business–oriented resource text that describes ABMS and then teaches

how to build simulations and apply them to business
decision–making)

64. For general overviews and examples of ABMS see:
   a. "Agent–based modeling: Methods and techniques for
      simulating human systems," E. Bonabeau, available
      at: www.pnas.org/content/99/suppl.3/7280.full
   b. "Predicting the Unpredictable—Can You Predict the
      Unpredictable?," E. Bonabeau, available at:
      http://hbswk.hbs.edu/archive/2934.html
   c. "Agent–based Modeling: A valuable new weapon for
      Chief Marketing Officer in the fight of their lives," the
      EMM Group, available at:
      www.decisionpower.com/news_and_events/pdf/AgentB
      asedModeling.pdf
   d. "An Agent–Based Model of the Airline Industry," W.
      Niedringhaus, available at:
      http://www.caasd.org/library/papers/ACSEM.pdf
   e. "The Aero–Engine Value Chain Under Future Business
      Environments: Using Agent–Based Simulation to
      Understand Dynamic Behavior," D. Buxton, R. Farr,
      and B. MacCarthy, available at:
      http://www.xjtek.com/file/10/
   f. "Agent–based modeling for competing firms: from
      balanced–scorecards to multiobjective strategies," T.
      Terano and K. Naitoh, available at:
      http://ieeexplore.ieee.org/xpl/freeabs_all.jsp?arnumber
      =1265251
65. A special issue focusing on Agent–Based Modeling of
    innovation: *The Journal of Product Innovation
    Management*, Product Development and Management
    Association, Volume 28, Number 2, March 2011.
66. For a description of participatory ABMS see: "Agent–Based
    Participatory Simulations: Merging Multi–Agent Systems
    and Role–Playing Games," P. Guyot and S. Honiden,
    available at: http://jasss.soc.surrey.ac.uk/9/4/8.html
67. Discusses different approached to decision–making:
    "Decision Making: It's Not What You Think," H. Mintzberg
    and F. Westley, *Sloan Management Review*, Spring, 2001
68. Perspectives on making change happen:

a. *"Leadership in a Combat Zone"* by W. Pagonis, Harvard Business Review, December 2001

b. *"The Secrets to Successful Strategy Execution"* by G. Neilson, K. Martin, and E. Powers, Harvard Business Review, June 2008

c. *"A Sense of Urgency"* by J. Kotter, Harvard Business Press, Boston, MA, 2008

d. *"The Execution Premium: Linking Strategy to Operations for Advantage"* by R. Kaplan and D. Norton, Harvard Business Press, Boston, MA, 2008.

Chapter 6

69. For books addressing business survival in difficult economic times see Reference (13) and:

a. *Chaotics – The Business of Managing and Marketing in the Age of Turbulence*, P. Kotler and J. Caslione, American Management Association 2009

b. *Beat the 2008 Recession: a Blueprint for Business Survival*, N. Gate, Infinite Ideas Limited, 2008

c. *Leadership in the Era of Economic Uncertainty: The New Rules for Getting the Right Things Done in Difficult Times*, R. Charan, McGraw–Hill, New York, NY, 2008

d. *Harvard Business Review on Leading in Turbulent Times*, Harvard Business School Press, Boston, MA, 2003

70. For good summary information on business survival see:

e. "Quick Tips: How to Recession–Proof Your Business," D. Ransom, available at: www.smsmallbiz.com/capital/How_to_Recession–Proof_Your_Business.html

f. "Smart Business for Tough Times," available at: www.bnet.com/2436–13241_23–251684.html

ABOUT THE AUTHORS

Dr. Carol Fatuzzo is the founder, President, and CEO of New Horizons Business Ventures, Inc. (NHBV). Prior to founding NHBV, Dr. Fatuzzo served as a Technical Director for 3M, one of the 100 largest US Manufacturing Corporations. Dr. Fatuzzo's professional career includes over 30 years of technical and leadership positions in a variety of global businesses. For more information about Dr. C. Fatuzzo, visit her Website: *nhbvinc.com.*

Dr. Ennio Fatuzzo is the President and CEO of EF Management Associates, Inc (EFMA). He is a seasoned corporate executive with extensive experience in managing large organizations, combating external business threats, and building synergy through acquisitions. Prior to EFMA, Dr. Fatuzzo founded and led AIM, Inc., an international business consulting company, and held business executive positions in 3M and other global enterprises. For more information about Dr. E. Fatuzzo, visit his Website: *efmainc.com.*

Together, the Fatuzzos also have written the book "DYNAMIC BUSINESS PLANNING BASICS", CreateSpace, 2010 (available in paperback and Kindle formats from Amazon.com).